At Home on This Moveable Earth

At Home on

This *Moveable* Earth

William Kloefkorn

University of Nebraska Press : Lincoln and London

Chapter 1 originally appeared in *The Iowa Review* (Summer 2005) under the title "At Home on This Movable Earth." Chapter 3 first appeared in *The Virginia Quarterly Review* 81, no. 3 (Summer 2005), under the title "Walking the Dog to Dover." A section of chapter 7, under the title "Down and Dirty: Re-visiting the Divine Fall," originally appeared in *Ascent* 28, no. 3 (Spring 2004). Chapter 11 originally appeared as "Afoot on This Movable Earth" in *New Letters* 71, no. 3 (Spring 2005). © 2005 by William Kloefkorn. Reprinted by permission of *New Letters* and the Curators of the University of Missouri–Kansas City. My special thanks to the editors of these periodicals.

Library of Congress Cataloging-in-Publication Data   Kloefkorn, William.   At home on this moveable earth / William Kloefkorn.   p. cm.   ISBN-13: 978-0-8032-2768-2 (cloth : alkaline paper)   ISBN-10: 0-8032-2768-x (cloth : alkaline paper)
1. Kloefkorn, William – Childhood and youth.   2. Poets, American – Homes and haunts – Kansas.   3. Poets, American – 20th century – Biography.   4. Kansas – Social life and customs.   5. Depressions – 1929 – Kansas.   6. Kloefkorn, William – Family.
7. Kansas—Biography.   I. Title   PS3561.L626Z464 2006   811'.54–dc22   2005026550

Special thanks to my brother
JOHNNY
whose generous spirit and keen
eye were, as always, invaluable

1

What I love is near at hand,
Always, in earth and air.
—Theodore Roethke, "The Far Field"

Most residents spend their lives without ever being affected
by a tornado – or ever observing one.
—F. C. Bates, "Tornadoes in the Central United States"

Track crews lived along and maintained each of the six- to
eight-mile sections into which the Santa Fe divided its line.
The crew would spend most of its day reinforcing weak
road-beds, tapping down loose pins, replacing worn ties,
and clearing the right-of-way of weeds, grass, and debris.
The foreman was also responsible for daily inspection of the
entire section. . . . [He] had to be a man of some experience
and common sense, but the track laborer needed little skill.
—James H. Ducker, *Men of the Steel Rails*

Calf bucket. Full to the brim with fresh, frothy milk, it's what my grandfather permitted me to carry from the cream separator out of the porch and around the house and across the backyard to the barbwire fence where under the lowest strand I would push it to feed the waiting calf. *Calf bucket*. It is also the rusty receptacle I found precisely where I had left it – near the lone stanchion in the barn near the alley, barn large enough to accommodate our one Jersey cow, barn with its weathered shingles and unpainted one-by-eights well on its way to oblivion.

We'll need another bucket to put the dirt in, my father had said. We already had one bucket, a discarded lard container Father had brought home from the cafe. But we needed another container so that as I trudged up the earthen steps to empty one, my father said, he could be filling the other.

I could sense that something big, maybe even something gargantuan, was about to unfold, but I didn't know exactly what that something might be. Early evening it was, and a Sunday. Mother was holding things down at the cafe, but on this particular Sunday Father was not there to help her. Instead, he was here at home, sporting a faded pair of blue overalls and a likewise faded blue work shirt with the sleeves rolled up beyond the elbows. In his right hand, the one with two middle fingers missing, he held the family shovel. When he told me to fetch the calf bucket I could see in his grass-green eyes a peculiar if not ominous triad of determination, anger, and spite.

The calf bucket had been given to me by my grandfather, perhaps because I had been playing with it and had asked if I might take it home, perhaps also because its sides were battered and its

3

bottom with half a dozen pinholes leaked milk somewhat on the order of a sieve. I had wanted it so desperately that once at home I had taken it to the barn where having placed it near the stanchion I promptly forgot why I had wanted it so desperately. But when I needed it there it was.

With the calf bucket in hand I followed my father into the screened-in porch at the southwest corner of the house, followed him over narrow tongue-and-groove boards to the door of our cave and storm shelter, door with its matching tongue-and-groove boards, door that lifted easily, thanks to a system of ropes and pulleys that the ten-year-old mind had, and to this day has, difficulty understanding. The earthen steps were dry and uneven; I took them one at a time, slowly, my father in front of me now balancing himself with the family shovel in his right hand and the lard can in the other.

Our cave was not a place conducive to a sense either of well-being or safety, in spite of the fact that we called it not only a cave, that word for us being synonymous with *a place for the storing of home-canned goods*, but likewise a storm shelter. Perhaps it somewhat fit Robert Frost's description of a home – that place where, when you have to go there, it has to take you in. Well, I cannot remember our ever having put our storm shelter to the test. I can remember many storms, thunder and hail and wind and sleet and snow, and I can remember hearing the intense and persistent whistle at the power plant telling us to take cover, but I cannot remember that we ever obeyed. For one thing, we were seldom all of us at home when the siren sounded. I and my younger brother and older sister might be in school, or busy separately with after-school activities, and more than likely Mother and Father would be at the cafe taking orders and dishing up bacon and eggs or hot-beef sandwiches. For another, none of us, I believe, wanted to de-

4

scend into the quaint fecundity of a dirt-walled, dirt-floored cave. You can the goods, yes, peaches and green beans and tomatoes and a varied assortment of jellies, and when you want a pint of this or a quart of something else you lift the cave door and feel your way down the uneven steps and with faith and doggedness and up-lifted hands you locate the string that when pulled will give you light, and because you forgot to bring a rag or a cloth you part the spider webs and dust off the jars with an open hand and make your selection; then, reversing the process, you retreat as quickly as possible.

And, finally, we did not resort to the storm shelter because my brother and I were eager to experience a tornado firsthand, to watch it and to feel its power to discern for ourselves whether it might be something more than hearsay or legend. When the siren sounded we would stop whatever we were doing and rush outside, if we weren't there already, and search the skies for anything re-motely resembling a funnel. Often we saw one, or thought so, and we would study it until the eyes burned, until in spite of rain and an impressive wind the funnel or its illusion lifted to join a roiling of blue-black clouds.

For me, an opportunity to witness a bona fide tornado would not present itself until I had graduated from junior high and was about to enter high school. Because I was not a whiz at mathemat-ics I often went to the Attica Recreation Parlor to learn the nu-ances of numbers by playing eightball. One late afternoon in late August I was deep into this learning process when the siren sounded. The sudden stridency did not altogether surprise me; all afternoon blue-black clouds had been forming to the southwest, and a stillness had hung in the air like a slow, silent, extended ex-pectation. But inside the pool hall, though the door that faced the main street was open, both clouds and expectation were replaced by the sweet acridity of cigarette smoke and the downright lovely clicking of one pool ball against another. Was I shooting the stripes or the solids? In this competition do any of the numbers except the eight on the black eight ball matter? And was I winning the game?

Probably, because my opponent was Frankie Biberstein, who had trouble with both angle and distance because one of his eyes wandered. Frankie would be a freshman, too, would be a junior if he had somewhere along the educational line applied himself.

Boy howdy, Frankie said. Must be a tornado.

So of course we racked our cues, paid our bill (ten cents per game, the winner receiving a five-cent redeemable chip for each victory), and hurried to Frankie's father's black and battered International pickup, which Frankie, using the eye that did not wander, drove like a madman west on Highway 160 to where the clouds appeared most threatening.

Frankie's father owned the pickup, but in all other respects it belonged to Frankie. On weekdays he drove it to school from his farm three miles west of town (that same direction we were now headed), and on Saturday nights he patrolled the streets as if he had been deputized – from the elevators at the south edge of Main to the school at the far north end, from the cemetery at the west edge to the town park at the east. He'd put the International in low gear and creep the streets from sundown until, as they say, the last dog died, the radio dialed to a clear-channel station from somewhere in Texas intoning news and music and ads for everything from lug nuts to noodles. My favorite was a come-on for engagement and wedding rings, one of each for under five dollars. Cheap enough to throw away, the baritone voice told us, but nice enough to keep.

The first time we heard that one Frankie almost drove us into the ditch. We had been moving beyond the speed limit, the windows up to keep the sound of the muffler from competing with the radio, and we were on our way to Anthony, sixteen miles away, to buy a brand of nuts not available in any of the local stores – Tom's Toasted Peanuts. Frankie enjoyed that sort of thing, something, anything, to give him an excuse to drive somewhere out of town, especially if he had someone to share his eccentricity. Often I served as that someone. Frankie was not very social, and he absolutely did not drive the streets of Attica hoping to catch the eye of a female. He was not altogether a loner, but he wanted to keep his relationships both few and at a distance. As an only child he had perhaps been doted upon and at the same time been given opportunities and responsibilities peculiar to a youngster being raised on a farm. Who knows how young he had been when he soloed on the family's row-crop Farmall, or how old he had been when he first sat behind the wheel of the old pickup.

Cheap enough to throw away, but nice enough to keep. He's talking about my International, Frankie had said, and probably it was this connection that had so nearly caused my buddy to chortle himself, and me with him, into the ditch.

Raindrops against the windshield were large but not plentiful, and the wipers at the moment were working. The blue-black clouds were flecked with white; they seemed to be turning slowly, and moving toward us, and shortly after we had navigated an S two miles from town and were again hauling our anxious little asses west, we saw the funnel.

Boy howdy, Frankie said, there she is!

In an instant Frankie had reined in the pickup, half of it resting on black macadam, the other half on the highway's shoulder. In another instant we were standing in the pickup's bed, looking west over the cab at what was no longer a legend. It was a funnel, all right, made not of tin or metal but of swirling winds that enabled it to bend this way and that as it moved its extended snout through a windbreak of cedars and cottonwoods at the south edge of the highway. It was maybe half a mile away, serpentining slowly, heading rather directly toward Frankie's old black International.

It never occurred to us that we might be in mortal danger – danger, yes, but not *mortal* danger. We were much too young to be mortality's victims. Had we been fully aware of the danger, we surely would have left the pickup running; but we hadn't. Frankie had turned her off, knowing that the pickup, chiefly because of temperamental carburetion, might not start quickly, or at all, should we decide to indulge what my Marine Corps handbook would call, as I learned many years later, a *retrograde movement.* Or maybe the scene had tricked us into believing that we were watching a movie, and that before long a cowboy wearing a wide-brimmed hat and riding a white horse – William Boyd, perhaps, as Hopalong Cassidy – would come into the picture at the last moment, lasso the funnel and take it to the ground and without losing his hat punch it silly. Or maybe we were improvising a version of chicken, Frankie and I equally unwilling to register fear, to back down, or to holler uncle.

In any case, there we stood, occasional raindrops the size of quarters pelting our faces, thanks to wind gusts from the southwest, and we wiped them away with the backs of our hands and watched as the funnel moved through the trees, parting them and leaving a swath wide enough, as later Frankie would put it, to drive half a dozen four-bottom plows through.

When suddenly the hum of the storm erupted into a terrific roar, I looked quickly at Frankie, who had turned quickly to look at me. There was an intensity in his better eye that bespoke more satisfaction than fear. Is it possible that he wanted to experience the funnel more fully than I did? Yes, I believe so, though I managed a difficult grin, which Frankie returned. Then he said something, probably something on the order of Boy howdy, here she comes! but the words were lost in the god-awful growl of the now not-so-distant maelstrom.

Only one other time in my life have I heard a sustained roaring to equal that of our approaching tornado. It came to me one summer when I was working as a gandy dancer on the Atchison, Topeka, and Santa Fe Railroad, Panhandle Division. I and my coworkers were replacing the nuts and bolts that secured the steel splices that held the rails together, and it was my job to swab the sides of the adjoining rails with grease before the splices with their new nuts and bolts were affixed. To perform this task I would dip a wide soft-bristled brush into a large bucket of melted grease, then give each side of the rails a long black sticky lovely coat. It was not a difficult job, not an intellectually challenging job, not one that any of my courses thus far in college (I would be a sophomore in the fall) had bothered to prepare me for, especially Beginning French, and fortunately the railroad job required a minimum of prerequisites – and accessories. One bucket. One brush. One back strong enough to tote the bucket.

One foreman capable of exercising compassion.

Case in point: the day I greased the tops, no less than the sides, of the tracks.

It had been an unusually hot day in early August, and by noon our foreman, Wilson, was unusually fatigued, which meant that shortly after lunch our foreman under a maverick cottonwood lay flat on his back, snoring, maybe dreaming of what he would say when after waking he would assemble his crew in a circle, insofar as four subalterns can form a circle, to present his weekly homily on the importance of railroad safety. Because of this: Ray Wilson believed in following the rules, in taking every precaution known to humankind to prevent injury or death to anyone in his care, his job no doubt equal to any humanitarian impulse hanging in the balance.

So when I looked up to see a green board – that is, a green orb of light high on a steel silver pole – warning that a train, most likely a freight, was about to pass, I decided to grease the tops of two parallel rails for say ten to fifteen feet, then stand well back to watch and thus determine the effect of the grease on the fast-moving train. The inspiration for this act did not strike me like a bolt from the blue, though the August skies were indeed blue and cloudless, nor did it reach me via one of the muses. Several days earlier one of my colleagues, Gene, had suggested that I do it, said that if I didn't I had shit down my neck, and a day or so later the challenge was repeated, feces included, so that eventually the dare had become the forbidden fruit that reached its irresistible maturity as our foreman lay on his back snoring under the disinterested cottonwood.

Well, I was young then, and to some extent fearless; I was the baby of our five-member crew, and to be honest I knew, down deep in my heart, that Ray liked me more than he should. He had one child, a daughter, and surely he loved her. But he wanted a son, too, or so I believed, because occasionally, if the context were appropriate, he would say to me, Now, if I had a son like you, I'd . . . And he would go on to tell me, and those others who might be nearby, what he'd do, and all the while he'd be looking at me as if I were in fact his son. He was a balding, large-chested man with amazingly short legs. Always he wore tan workpants and a blue cotton shirt. Always black low-topped boots. Always a growth of whiskers that somehow, unlike the forbidden fruit, never reached full maturity. And always, unless asleep, snoring, he wore a straw hat with an impressively wide brim.

I began and continued the job as quietly and as swiftly as I could. One bucket of grease. One soft-bristled brush. One back strong enough to tote the bucket. Were my co-laborers watching, most importantly the one who had tossed out, then repeated, the dare? This would be Gene, who helped Mr. Shaw manipulate the machine that removed then replaced the nuts and the bolts. Or would the oldest member of the crew, Joseph Mora, our welder who beaded the worn-down ends of the rails, take notice? He was a dark, quiet, bright-eyed man who chuckled at almost everything, maybe because he did not speak our English very well, but who seldom laughed outright.

I did not bother to notice or to care whether anyone might be watching. I was coating the tops of the tracks with black sticky lovely goo. I was light as cottonwood seed on water as I moved over the ties and the chat, swabbing. Heat ascended in discernible waves from the rails. Not much of a breeze. A rivulet of warm moisture under my T-shirt teased the spine. The green eye continued to offer its warning.

I finished in less time than it takes here to tell it, and when looking west I saw the light on the engine moving starboard and port, searching the rights-of-way, and heard the rumbling, I wondered if indeed I had done something destined now to destroy us all, including the engineer and his misbegotten helper. In a flash I imagined the huge front wheels of the locomotive hitting the grease and spinning suddenly more rapidly than tongue might tell or pen inscribe, imagined sparks flying as the engine jumped the tracks, countless cars huge as ogres following suit, imagined one of those massive ogres hurtling toward me, toward Gene, toward Mr. Shaw, toward Joseph, toward our snoring foreman, imagined . . .

You must understand that the approaching train was an old-fashioned study in raw power and motion, a coal-fed, steam-powered behemoth with "ponderous sidebars, parallel and connecting rods," as Walt Whitman phrases it in "To a Locomotive in Winter." A "fierce-throated beauty" belching smoke thick as clouds from its smokestack, the "pulse of the continent," according to Whitman, and certainly I did not disagree because, for one thing, I had not yet read Walt Whitman and, for another, Whitman knew what he was talking about.

Now the rumbling swelled in a mighty crescendo as the freight, relentless and black as midnight, lurched menacingly toward us. O sweet, sweet Jesus! I have sinned and have fallen hellishly short of God's glory. On the other hand, I have not backed away from my coworker's challenge. Dead or alive, damned or saved, I do not have shit down my neck.

Roar and heft: Both were upon us as the engineer, smiling broadly, waved a gloved hand toward us as if he were a gleeful Pontiff in overalls offering a blessing. With the exception of our foreman, who remained asleep, we smiled and waved back.

You must understand also that the time that elapsed between the waving and the contact of the huge front wheels with the black sticky lovely grease was less than a millisecond, which means that the change on the countenance of the engineer from gladness to abject fright was too rapid to have been recorded by any contraption less sensitive than the naked eye. In a twinkling this convivial Pontiff went from paradise to the lowest reaches of perdition, and with the naked eye I observed the change and was impressed. The locomotive's huge wheels spun in place for only the smallest fraction of a moment, and sparks flew, but neither the engine nor any of the countless boxcars jumped the tracks. In another twinkling the wheels found their familiar because goo-less purchases and the freight rumbled safely on, its clickety-clacking like music to the ears, its engineer no doubt trying to remember which of his forgotten transgressions could have provoked the skipping of such an otherwise regular heartbeat.

Apparently my fellow workers had not seen me greasing the tracks, because when our foreman regained consciousness and found his legs and asked us what the hell was going on (the skipping of the heartbeat must have roused him, must have given him a hint), we said, I believe collectively, damned if we knew. It's nothing to lose any sleep over, we said, I believe ironically, just another freight with maybe a novice engineer at the controls, or more likely one of the wheels was going flat.

Our foreman tilted and shook his head as if he had water in one ear, and when the water was gone he put on his straw hat and closed his lunch bucket and told us to sit down here under this goddamned cottonwood in a goddamned circle and listen up. Said he knew we didn't much care to hear him talk again about railroad safety, but rules are rules, he said, and I believe in following the goddamned rules, and that includes rules on railroad safety, he said, and I could tell from the way he said it, soft spoken and intense with his eyes aimed at me, that I was the only son he'd ever have, and that goddamn it he loved me, and that meant he had to forgive me for whatever it was I might have done or one day in the sweet by-and-by might better not, by God, by Jesus H. Christ, ever think of doing.

"We call the moon the moon," John Donne wrote, and I write that we call human nature human nature because it's what we don't stop doing – so it must be in our nature to do it, then do it again, advice and caution and dictates to the contrary notwithstanding. When you see a green board, Ray Wilson says each time we huddle to hear his speech, and we hear it weekly, you shout *Green board!* then you drop whatever you're doing and help pissant the motorcar off the tracks, assuming it ain't already off. I don't want anybody's injury or death on my record, or on my conscience, either. And in unison we nod *yes*, we nod *yesyesyes*, and after a prolonged silence, intended to permit our foreman's words to sink deeply in, we break huddle and return to work.

There are many ways to injure or destroy oneself while working on the railroad. A lining bar, for example, might slip and fracture a bone in the ankle. The business end of a sledgehammer might miss the spike and shatter the tibia. Ray Wilson once spoke of a man who was killed when the head of a sledgehammer came loose and flew a good twenty-five feet and struck the unwary victim squarely between the eyes and killed him more or less instantly. Our foreman was not present when this happened, he said, but he said he had it on good authority. And of course there was always the possibility of being struck by a motorcar. And you don't look directly at Joe Mora's welder when he is laying a bead. Keep your eyes and your ears open, Wilson tells us, and you'll not be injured or killed and I'll not get my ass fired or find myself sitting around feeling guilty.

Even so, we call the moon the moon. And human nature is human nature, which translated means that none of us, not even Wilson, was keeping his eyes and ears open that late afternoon when a freight train materialized so suddenly that by Mr. Shaw's estimate, given not long after we survived, we had six point five seconds to remove our machines and tools and ourselves from the tracks to avoid total annihilation.

We reacted instinctively, instinct augmented by our foreman's many lectures on railroad safety. Gene and Mr. Shaw removed their machine from the tracks in a single inclusive motion. Joseph threw both torch and mask into the adjoining county and jumped perhaps fifty feet to safety. I threw my bucket with its brush into the stratosphere and duplicated Joseph's leap.

These movements – of Mr. Shaw and Gene, of Joseph and myself – took approximately three seconds, during which time Ray was racing to the motorcar, leaving him three point five seconds to wrestle it off the rails and heave it far enough onto the right-of-way to keep it from being sideswiped and maybe snagged by one of the freight's appendages and dragged all the way to Alva, Oklahoma.

History abounds with stories of heroes, often mythical and god-related, performing feats of incredible physical prowess. Homer's Odysseus, for all his brawn and brain, could not have cleaned house so thoroughly without Athena beside him, whispering encouragement into his mortal ear. And surely Aeneas's and his henchmen's conquest of Italy by way of Turnus would have been delayed, nay prevented, without the ongoing intervention of his goddess mother, Venus. These figures were burly to start with, and when they had the favor of a god or goddess they were impervious to damn near everything. So one might reasonably expect them to slay whatever form of dragon that blocked their paths.

But what does one expect of the average individual, the person on the street as common as dirt? Not Odysseus or Aeneas, not even Davy Crockett or his multitudinous equivalents. I am thinking instead of the one without badge or reputation, the one who when the chips are down does whatever must be done to prevail.

Certainly, Ray Wilson was such a man. When collectively we heard the train's whistle, and in unison looked up from our respective involvements, the freight was upon us, and it was our foreman, Ray Wilson, who without benefit of god or goddess performed his Herculean duty. In an instant his amazingly short legs became pistons to deliver him to the motorcar. In another instant he pulled the set-off handles from their slots at one end of the car, lifted that near end off the rails and dropped it on the crushed rocks that provided a bed for the ties. Earlier, I admitted that I have never been much of a mathematician, though in the pool hall playing rotation I practiced the difficult art of simple addition. What I am saying is that I do not know how many instants make a second; I know only that our foreman, having lifted one end of the motorcar off the rails, proceeded in another instant to move to the other end of the car, which now rested on ties and chat between the rails, then lifted the vehicle's dead squat weight and pushed it like a Brobdingnagian wheelbarrow down the mound of chat and onto the right-of-way, the locomotive as it passed him not missing the timetable in his right rear pocket by more than a whisker. I know this because as we sat in a circle to indulge a debriefing Mr. Shaw said so.

Missed your ass-end by a whisker, Ray, said Mr. Shaw.

Wilson did not respond. He sat with his amazingly short legs crossed, his back straight as a rake handle, his round cherubic face white as flour. He resembled an ancient Oriental god scared, as someone later noted, shitless. The debriefing had been his idea, yet thus far he had said nothing.

Mr. Shaw did most of the talking. He was the crew clock-watcher, having told us that the entire episode lasted six point five seconds. Mr. Shaw went on to say that each of us was to blame equally, that hereafter we should be more vigilant, that he simply could not understand why one of us did not see the green board or hear the whistle, if the freight had blown one, or why the engineer hadn't applied the brakes, or how during those frantic six point five seconds our foreman's straw hat had managed to remain on our foreman's head, or . . .

16

During all of this Joe Mora sat smiling, off and on, or softly giggling; with his welder's mask removed he looked younger than probably he was.

I joined Gene in saying nothing. Mr. Shaw had pretty much taken over, his spontaneous verbal leadership perhaps providing another form of heroism.

After a long, long string of instants Ray reached a hand behind him and from a hip pocket brought forth his dog-eared timetable, which for another interminable string of instants he studied as we studied him. Then: She was right on time, he said. It was my fault. I should have checked the timetable earlier.

No one responded, because we knew that Ray was being flat out honest; we did in fact often depend upon him to advise us of an impending train. He took enormous satisfaction in studying his timetable, almost as much satisfaction in the timetable as in the motorcar. As foreman he read the schedule as if decoding messages from a band of secret agents. As foreman he alone started the motorcar and manipulated the upright handle that tightened the belt that put the car in motion. He therefore as the keeper of both timetable and motorcar was finally responsible for the safety of his crew, though of course each crew member was advised and encouraged to keep an eye out for the green board.

But we call the moon the moon, don't we, and we call human nature human nature because it's what we don't stop doing – so it must be in our nature to do it, then do it again, warnings and so forth be damned.

That day we did not return to work. We instead located our equipment and machines, examined then covered them with a tarp, returned the motorcar to the tracks and with our foreman at the helm navigated the tracks west and then south to Alva, where we were living in boxcars too hot to get much sleep in, it being early August in Oklahoma – and in Kansas also, that pitiful state where I was born and where I couldn't wait to get back to.

As the funnel came slowly nearer, the decibels of its roaring increasing steadily, Frankie and I stood on our toes in the bed of his International, not wanting to miss anything. I suppose that by now we had reached a point of no return, that without saying it we had determined to live or die watching the tornado.

Frankie had stopped the International at the top of a small rise, a place from which we had a panoramic view of the proceedings, a spectacular view made an inch or two more spectacular because, as I noted, we were standing on our toes. The rain had slacked off as the wind increased, and the growl in the throat of the tornado was becoming downright personal. The business end of the funnel was moving through the windbreak with an appalling absence of mercy, reducing cottonwood and cedar to fiddlesticks and stumps. The scene was much too unreal to have been believed, and maybe that is why Frankie and I did not retreat. Like voyeurs, or certifiable idiots, we stood on tiptoes, our hands palms-down on the cab of the pickup, our hearts beating like tom-toms in our throats.

Where the windbreak ended is precisely where the funnel turned slowly northward and began to lift. The scenario was exactly the way Frankie and I would have planned it, had we been the one, or One, in charge. The funnel, rising, crossed the highway beyond and below us and continued north, rising and rising, until it dissipated and joined the blue-blackness that now began to drop its rain on Frankie and me in buckets.

We sat then in the pickup, which had surprised us by starting, until the rain let up, and because the wipers worked Frankie suggested we drive west all the way to Sharon, nine miles, to rubberneck the damage. So we did. But there was nothing much to see beyond the shredding of the windbreak, unless you happened to own the hangar or its blue-and-white piper cub near the southside city limits. The top of the hangar was lying crumpled on the runway, and the piper cub lay upside down in a field of stubble that was waiting to be plowed.

We drove the main street and several side streets, the rain steady but slackening, the radio on, static and country western, and when we started home and drove past the unfortunate piper cub Frankie said, Cheap enough to throw away, but nice enough to keep. On the radio "Texas" Jim Robertson was singing "Land, Sky, and Water," a song that disparages tall buildings and streets and sidewalks teeming with humanity, and in their stead praises open prairies with their rolling pastures, clear-water streams, and high blue skies.

We had all three, did Frankie and I. Boy howdy. In addition, we had firsthand information about a tornado that folks back home in the pool hall would be anxious to hear – you know, those folks who had not seen the devastation with their own eyes, those weak-kneed pismires who might live the rest of their lives without ever knowing the sound of a bona fide tornado in their ears.

When finally I asked my father what he was about to do, he seemed surprised that I didn't already know.

Install a floor furnace, he said, and apparently he assumed that no further explanation was necessary. I had trailed him down the earthen steps to the earthen floor of our cave, our storm shelter, had hesitated while he found the dangling string and with the family shovel in his right hand pulled the string; light from the lone bulb was barely adequate, giving everything – the jars of canned goods, the glints of mica – a faintly yellowish, almost sickly, hue. And the smell – it was decidedly that of a place not very often used, dry and stale with now and then the suggestion of something putrid, potatoes, probably, gone bad, but the funny thing is that it never took me very long to adjust to these unpleasant odors. Over time, over the days and weeks that it took my father and me to complete our project, I adjusted to the scents so completely that I came to enjoy them.

Meanwhile, observe the scene: A man wearing faded blue overalls and a blue, ragbag cotton shirt is standing, facing the earthen center of the south wall. In his right hand he holds a short-handled shovel. At his right, on the earthen floor, sits a calf bucket, its sides replete with dents, its bottom a punchboard of pinholes. Behind the bucket stands a boy of ten or so, waiting for something that he does not yet fully understand to begin.

It begins when his father strikes the earthen side of the cave with the blade of his shovel. One blow, then another, and the boy counts the blows until he loses track, and he loses track when the father, having filled the calf bucket with dry dirt, tells him to carry the load upstairs and dump it on that patch of bunchgrass just east of the outhouse, then bring the calf bucket back and trade it for the lard can, which, if it isn't full by the time he returns, will be full pretty damned shortly thereafter.

Not full, as it turns out, not ever completely full, but half full, because the lard can is too large for the boy to negotiate unless he drags it, and dragging would wear down the earthen steps; so half full, or thereabouts, is the extent to which the father fills the lard can, and the boy carries it up the earthen steps and out of the porch to dump it on that patch of bunchgrass just east of the outhouse, returns then to await the filling of another container.

It takes the boy a long time to realize that this is the way it is going to be, that one small load at a time he will carry earth up the earthen steps to dump it near the outhouse, that he will return to the cave to watch his father chip away at the south wall of the cave, that his father by Christ will not relent, that his father's green eyes are indeed a triad of determination, anger, and spite, that if after an impossible stretch of days and weeks you carry calf bucket and lard can up and down the earthen steps so many times that not even your younger brother, who loves math, he says, could count them you notice that the pile of dirt near the outhouse is beginning to resemble first a mound, then a hill, then a mountain – you come to the conclusion that, yes, you and your father, come hell or high water, are indeed going to install a floor furnace.

2

One leg over the other the dog walks to Dover.
                              —British lore

Let me not to the marriage of true minds
Admit impediments. Love is not love
Which alters when it alteration finds,
Or bends with the remover to remove . . .
                              —William Shakespeare, Sonnet 116

When the hill of dirt that had been a mound became a mountain, and the wall that my father chipped away at became a passageway three feet wide with its sides very neatly sloped to discourage a cave-in, tedium turned to mild anticipation, and by early October anticipation yielded to feverish excitement. And I noticed that the anger in my father's grass-green eyes had gone away, and with it the narrowness I had seen as spite. You see, he was hell-bent on installing the floor furnace because his wife, my mother, was hell-bent on having him do it. She was not altogether a nag; she was a woman sick to the death, as she put it again and again, of spending winter in a house heated with a Warm Morning coal stove, sick to the death of being overly hot in the room where the stove was and overly chilly in all the other rooms. Was there any wonder that she and the kids had coughs and runny noses all winter long?

But we didn't have much money, certainly not enough to afford hiring someone to do the work, from start to finish, and my father did not have the expertise to do the final installation; he knew how to handle a shovel, how to fill one container then another (one to the top, the other half way), and how to shave the sides of the passageway to make it safe for him and his son to travel. So driven by that trinity of determination, anger, and spite he set out to do whatever he could and to hell with the final installation. He would cross that bridge should one day he come to it.

He might have thought, If I am going to break my infernal back with this infernal shovel at least I'll know who's to blame. And perhaps this thought gave him enough devilish pleasure to drive him on. He might have thought, as I did for a long time, that eventually Mother would see the futility of the project and call it off, tell him she was wrong and now she is sorry and the old Warm Morning stove really isn't all that bad, after all. Or he might have had more confidence in himself than I give him credit for, might have foreseen the successful end to the cockeyed project from the moment he first poked the dirt wall with the family shovel.

I do believe, though, that as the passageway evolved, inch into foot into another foot, his anger and spite evaporated in direct proportion to the rising of his confidence. I first noticed the change when, returning to the cave from the dirt pile near the outhouse, I heard him whistling "The Great Speckled Bird." He was not an accomplished whistler, but on those rare occasions when he whistled he did it with a quiet intensity that suggested contentment. Then once in a while, if the contentment were deep enough, he would hum or sing a swatch of what he had been whistling. *What a beautiful thought I am thinking, concerning the great speckled bird.* His repertoire was not extensive – "The Great Speckled Bird," probably his favorite, "The Wabash Cannonball" and, later, "Satisfied Mind."

And the ditty that derived from the collecting of Raleigh coupons.

My father smoked cigarettes, mostly Camels and Lucky Strikes, but he shifted to Raleighs for several years because he wanted to collect then redeem their coupons. He kept the coupons rubberbanded and in plain sight atop the buffet in the dining room, and I watched the small packet become a large one as my father rather quickly depleted one pack of Raleighs after another. How could he afford such a smoky extravagance? I don't know. Maybe because he sold them in the cafe, before they were rationed during the war, and he could buy them wholesale, or maybe he kept one of his grass-green eyes out for empty discarded packages. What I do know is that the wad of coupons grew larger and larger, prompting me to wonder when if ever my father was going to redeem them – and for what? We needed many things, according to Mother – an indoor toilet, a new Maytag, a softer mattress for my older sister's rock-hard bed. But I had difficulty imagining any of these arriving in the mail as a consequence of my father's redeeming his Raleigh coupons, though I wanted to believe, and I tried desperately to believe, that in this veil of tears anything under the sun was possible.

The sad truth is that he never did redeem them. We therefore continued to frequent the outhouse, all of us, in both torrid and arctic weather, and Mother continued to humor our ancient Maytag, to feed our shirts and pants and blouses into wringers that occasionally clogged, and my sister continued to sleep on a mattress that she said was like sleeping on bricks, though I do not believe she had ever slept on bricks. I meanwhile – and sometimes my brother with me – hefted the packet of coupons, counted them, wondered what miracle might come to us should our father one day redeem them.

The Raleigh ditty, or what I thought of as the Raleigh ditty, probably was not connected to the Raleigh cigarettes that my father so faithfully smoked. It went like this: *I'm saving up coupons to buy one of those. A coupon redeemer, I'll die, I suppose.* One of those. What did that mean, *one of those*? New outhouse? New Maytag? New mattress? Or, perhaps most likely, a carton of free cigarettes? But if it meant free cigarettes, why the reference to death? Didn't that suggest a rather ominous cause-effect relationship? Yes, it did, meaning that, no, the ditty probably wasn't a commercial for Raleighs. It must have come from a source I could not pin down.

In any event, the tune that carried the words was a pleasant one, and when my father put tune and words together I knew that at least for the moment he was enjoying a satisfied mind.

Another case in point: the day I threw my girlfriend's lunch bucket into Mabel Cleveland's cow lot.

I was fond of Virginia Mae Prindle. I was older than when I helped my father install a floor furnace, but I was not yet old enough to understand any of the complexities of human passion. I could react to it. I could look at Virginia Mae's moon-shaped face and into her cerulean eyes and realize that something important was going on, or about to, inside my overalls. She was maybe a trifle on the pudgy side, pudgy being the word my mother used to describe anyone with an ample waistline. But ampleness on Virginia Mae only made her more desirable, I believe because she did not seem to be aware of it. She giggled easily, and frequently, and her teeth were white and even, and her hair was corn silk.

Because I was shy I didn't know how to convey my feelings. I could talk to her, yes, and I often did as we walked to school together. She lived over there and I lived over here, and two or three times a week our paths crossed coincidentally and we strolled to school together, she with her yellow lunch bucket and I with my lunch in a brown paper sack. We were in the same class, Miss Yoder's, and each morning to settle us into first period Miss Yoder would read for ten or fifteen minutes from Fenimore Cooper's *Last of the Mohicans*. Perhaps Virginia Mae and I would say something about the book, somebody being captured and someone else pursuing the captors, or maybe we would talk about an assignment that had given us trouble; but until that morning in early May we did not talk about any of the several complexities of human passion.

Nor did we talk about it that particular morning. But for reasons I didn't understand I wanted to convey to Virginia Mae, through some means other than words, how deeply into my soul my fondness for her reached. I now realize that my shyness was

doing battle with what is sometimes called *biological determinism.*
And it came to this: That early morning in May, a morning bright
with sunshine and lively with birdsong, shyness and biological determinism stood toe-to-toe with their gloves on, and shyness was
knocked flat on its back before it could deliver a single punch.
Overcome suddenly by biological determinism, I seized Virginia
Mae's yellow lunch bucket before she had so much as a mini-in-
stant to protest, and with strength that must have been provided
by the same force that one day would enable Ray Wilson to man-
handle his motorcar off the rails and onto the right-of-way I threw
her bucket over a nearby fence and well into the heart of Mabel
Cleveland's cow lot.

For roughly an eternity we stood looking at each other, Virginia
Mae's cerulean eyes those skies you want to become stars in. On
her moon-shaped face was a look of utter bewilderment. Then, as
if being touched in the ribs by some invisible muse, she began to
smile, a slight upturn at the corners of her lovely mouth that soon
became a full-blown smile that parted her lips to reveal her white,
perfectly even teeth. It was a smile no less of delight than of understanding. I could see it in both the smile and the cerulean eyes. She
understood, and she understood absolutely. Without words her
countenance was saying, You did this only for me, Billy Kloefkorn.
You must love me very much, so much that you seized my yellow
lunch bucket and threw it into Mabel Cleveland's cow lot. I am a
very lucky girl to have such a man of action love her, and I love
you, too.

True love, of course, is a very difficult thing to explain, especially to those who have not yet had the good fortune to experience it. True love, as the lyrics of a song will one day phrase it, is
that feeling you feel when you're feeling a feeling you've never felt
before. And that's exactly how I felt as I stood watching Virginia

Mae watching me. Both of us understood, and we understood absolutely. Then, after the eternity had passed, we walked on to school, silent but fulfilled, as meanwhile the yellow lunch bucket lay at the center of Mabel Cleveland's cow lot, its lid open and its contents scattered beautifully among the greening grass and the cow pies.

Nor did the feeling go away during the first period as Miss Yoder began another chapter of *Last of the Mohicans*. If anything, her reading from that book enhanced the feeling, because now all of the heroines in the book were in fact Virginia Mae, all of them moon-faced with cerulean eyes and corn silk for hair and white, even teeth, all of them appropriately pudgy, and those attempting to rescue them were likewise appropriately pudgy, all of them in fact myself. And the prairies and the forests through which the captors fled and the good guys pursued were in fact one immense cow lot at the center of which lay Virginia Mae's yellow lunch bucket.

I could envision that scene, and all that it portended, as clearly as if it were there in the classroom before me. The yellow lunch bucket, its top jarred open upon impact. A white-bread sandwich. An apple. A thermos. A few pieces of candy, lemon drops or a jaw-breaker, perhaps, or a stick of red or black licorice. And I could see the bewilderment in the eyes of Mabel Cleveland's Holstein standing near the trunk of a mulberry tree, after observing something yellow and foreign falling from the sky. O how she must have reached far back into the darkest recess of her bovine memory in an effort to explain such a phenomenon, and how, having reached back, she found no answer. And I felt sorry for the poor cow, sorry because being alone she had no one with whom to share her epiphany, no other milk cow to hear her story and with her reach a satisfying, maybe even theological, conclusion. Is there a heaven for milk cows? There must be. And what must the milk cow do to get there? Or to be sainted? Surely the viewing of a yellow foreign object falling from the sky constitutes a legitimate milk cow miracle. Saint Holstein, who, having witnessed the miracle, proceeded to nibble at its contents, apple and candy and white-bread sandwich quaint as the contents of any miracle can be on the lips.

Nor did the feeling go away as we sat in the basement of our little school eating lunch. We had separated ourselves, as people do, in the following manner: Those girls with lunch buckets sat at a table near the west wall. Those boys with lunch buckets sat at a table near the east wall. Those girls with sack lunches sat discreetly near the girls with lunch buckets. Those boys with sack lunches sat discreetly near the boys with lunch buckets. Those who could afford hot lunches went through the lunch line and sat wherever they damn well pleased.

From my vantage point near the east wall I could look beyond my open sack and across the room to see Virginia Mae sitting with her friends, a trace of delight and understanding lingering on her lips. She had no lunch to eat, yet from where I sat she seemed almost divinely satisfied, maybe even a trifle smug. She was being looked at quizzically by her colleagues, and she was fielding what must have been a compelling variety of questions.

Why don't you have anything to eat, Virginia Mae?

I lost my lunch bucket.

No you didn't.

Yes I did.

Where did you lose it, Virginia Mae?

Somewhere.

You did not. Where?

Somewhere.

Where is somewhere?

31

Well, that's for me to know and for you to find out.

And so on and on until, I'm guessing, Virginia Mae by degrees loosened her lovely lips and by degrees such hints as *cow lot* and *Cleveland* and *Billy what's-his-name* dribbled forth until eventually all of the beans had been spilled and everyone in Harper County, including my mother, learned pretty much what had happened.

That evening therefore I found myself walking beside my father as we made our way in the general direction of Mabel Cleveland's cow lot. Would the yellow lunch bucket still be there? Yes, probably, because Virginia Mae, though she knew little or nothing about the myriad niceties of chivalric romance, would not have demeaned herself by crawling through the barbwire fence to retrieve the bucket herself. And though it was possible that someone else might have rescued the lunch bucket, it was not very probable.

Mother, who also knew little or nothing about the chivalric romance, did not find any of this amusing, so she had more or less ordered my father to go with me to the cow lot to supervise my retrieving the lunch bucket, and then, she said, you go with your son straight to Virginia Mae's house where you see to it that your son returns the lunch bucket and apologizes for what he did.

To a certain degree, then, my father was no less under the gun than I was. Even so, I feared that beneath his outwardly placid exterior something highly volatile might be waiting for precisely the right moment to explode. And if it did what might he say? What might he do?

Using a full moon as a flashlight I crawled between two strands of barbwire being forced wide apart by my father's left foot and the thumb and two fingers on his right hand. He had not uttered one word as we walked from the cafe to the fence, nor had I; we might have been on night patrol deep inside enemy territory so silently did we negotiate the gravel road. The early evening was windless, the sweet scents of early spring at odds with our mission, though I must add that the mission was not altogether unsavory. True, my father at any moment might erupt, and the thought of delivering the lunch bucket into the hands of Virginia Mae, or her mother or father, was not too appealing. But these were surface concerns, very real but very transitory. What truly mattered was my knowing that Virginia Mae understood and would appreciate forever the motive behind the seizing and the tossing of the lunch bucket. In college my French professor, Dr. Minnie M. Miller, will one day label this motive *demand d'amour*, and I will nod my head knowingly, recalling Virginia Mae.

The open lunch bucket was there at the center of the lot, its thermos lying nearby, its other contents scattered, probably having been nibbled at by Mabel Cleveland's Holstein. I placed the thermos inside the bucket, snapped shut the lid, and returned to where my father again helped me through the barbwire fence.

For some reason I can't explain I somehow knew that it would be Mr. Prindle who would answer my knock at the door. Mr. Prindle was a hulk, silent and inscrutable. He filled every inch of the doorway. His face was square and in need of a shave. It showed no trace of human emotion.

I had walked up three or four wooden steps to stand on a floor of unpainted pine – tongue-and-groove, like the back porch of my house, except that the Prindle porch was not screened in. My father had not followed me. He had stopped at the foot of the steps and now he stood there, his hands in the pockets of his blue overalls, waiting.

Mr. Prindle said, Yes? He was in his undershirt.

I looked up. Mr. Prindle was huge. The doorway fit him like a medieval cloak. Before opening the door he had switched on the porch light, a yellow bulb that now made him appear jaundiced.

We were separated by a screen door that had been repaired in several places with white adhesive tape.

This is Virginia Mae's lunch bucket, I said. I'd like to return it.

Mr. Prindle looked down at the bucket, then slowly, as I shuffled backward, he pushed open the screen door.

I threw it over a barbwire fence into Mabel Cleveland's cow lot, I said. This morning, on our way to school. I lifted the yellow container toward Mr. Prindle's awesome chest.

Mr. Prindle said, Oh?

I did it just for fun, I said. I'm sorry. I'll try not to do it again.

Mr. Prindle continued to study the yellow lunch bucket. Its yellow was enhanced by the glow from the yellow porch light.

My arm was growing tired. I looked back over my left shoulder to see my father standing like a poorly trained sentry at the foot of the porch steps. Where was Virginia Mae? Where was her mother? When if ever was Mr. Prindle going to take the lunch bucket?

It was a scene that any artist worth a tinker's damn would love to have painted – a boy holding a yellow lunch bucket only inches from the chest of a Goliath, the boy's face in partial profile, wide-eyed with apprehension, the face of the Goliath jaundiced and noncommittal, the tongue-and-groove boards on the floor of the porch jaundiced, too, the boy's father standing at the foot of the steps, waiting, a full May moon in stasis between the roof of the house and an elm tree that, like the moon, probably wasn't there.

At last, without any expression beyond a nod of his head, Mr. Prindle took the lunch bucket. I lowered my arm, which was becoming numb. Before retreating, I watched Mr. Prindle back away and close the door. Soon thereafter the yellow bulb went out.

We were maybe half way home when my father began to whistle, softly, and then just as softly began to sing: *I'm saving up coupons to buy one of those . . .*

I had heard him sing this ditty before, it and bits and pieces of "The Great Speckled Bird" and "The Wabash Cannonball." It meant that his mind was satisfied, and this meant that nothing inside him just now was volatile, or, if it was, it had been defused. It meant that his errant son was off the hook. It meant that the father too was off the hook, that the father's wife would be happy to learn that father and son, together, had performed their respective acts of responsibility and contrition.

A coupon redeemer, I'll die, I suppose.

I suppose. But not just now. Just now there is maybe a full moon rising, the face of Virginia Mae rising, and there are three more blocks of gravel road to be walked upon, lightly, as if its makeup were water, before we return safely home.

When I returned to the cave that day with an empty calf bucket I could hear my father singing, the words barely audible because he was deep into the tunnel that he and the family shovel were carving. *What a beautiful thought I am thinking, concerning the great speckled bird.* He was deep into the tunnel, having dug far enough to the south and now, having turned a corner, was shoveling his way east. And I believe that it was the rounding of the corner that bolstered his confidence and, in turn, bolstered mine. Until then he had neither hummed nor sung anything. He had faced the wall of dirt as if confronting something both ugly and personal, as if the confrontation were too deadly serious to permit the slightest show of merriment. It had taken us several weeks to turn this corner because we did not work regularly; my father was devoted to the cafe from early morning until late at night, and I spent most of my time in school or studying comic books or fussing, or playing, with my brother, whose favorite game of late was King of the Mountain, mountain being the mound of dirt just east of the outhouse. And maybe that rising mound was another reason for my optimism, for my believing that yes, sure enough, this family might live long enough to see this project completed. Boy howdy.

My father was working now under a light provided by an extension cord, his off-and-on singing made deeply resonant because of his confinement. I would walk the tunnel to where he was digging, calf bucket or lard container in hand, and I would trade one bucket for another, or wait for a bucket to be filled or half-filled, and I could stand on my toes and look into the crawl space and smell its mustiness, and I could see the undersides of the boards that were the floors of our rooms and the top of our tunnel, boards with many nails protruding, could see the two-by-sixes that held the boards and, watching my father dig, sometimes kneeling, sometimes standing, and now sometimes humming or singing, I forgot completely the triad of anger, resolution and spite that I believed I had seen in my father's eyes when he began the project.

Frequently my brother helped me with the buckets, which gave both of us more time to stand in the tunnel and absorb its ambiance. Johnny was small for his age, and would be until his final year of high school, but he was tenacious – *feisty* is the word our mother preferred, and some years later as I read William Faulkner's "The Bear" with its small, wiry dog, its feist, refusing to back down as it confronted the bear, I will think of my feisty brother with his teeth bared lugging a bucket of Kansas dirt across the floor of the cave and up the steps and out of the porch and across the driveway to add it to the impending mountain just east of the outhouse, mountain he'll stand atop of to proclaim himself King – until his older and larger brother with the force of an entire Mongolian horde ascends the mountain and executing a flanking movement kicks the ass of his feisty but smaller and younger brother squarely into the middle of next Wednesday.

But it was my younger brother who one late afternoon in October said, No more coal. And I said, No more coal? And he said, If we have a furnace we won't need any more coal.

Jesus. This simple realization had never occurred to me, but it was true: If we were to finish the project before winter set in, and the possibility now seemed likely, we would no longer need coal, or a coal bucket in which to load it before dragging it into the house to set it beside the old Warm Morning stove.

Johnny grinned. No more coal. Now whisper it, Johnny, this time in terms that our father might truly appreciate and understand. No more *goddamned* coal.

Coal is dirty and smelly and heavy and difficult to load into a bucket, especially difficult if one is wearing a heavy coat and cumbersome gloves and a stocking cap (whisper it, Johnny, a *goddamned* stocking cap) and the wind is blowing and so is the snow and the pile of coal is seventeen miles from the house covered with snow beside a tool shed that has almost no tools in it, only a couple of milk buckets and a defunct cream separator and some ancient odds and ends that no one you know of can identify, or would care to. It is the shed from which you took the family shovel to confront for the first time this winter the pile of coal, shovel you will not return to the tool shed until winter is absolutely over, shovel meanwhile you use to fill the coal bucket you know will need to be refilled before you can say Jack Robinson because the Warm Morning stove will devour it like a famished beast and there you go again out to the *goddamned* coal pile . . .

The winter before the advent of the floor furnace, Johnny and I devised a plan whereby we hoped to make the loading of the coal bucket swift and painless, thus reducing the odds of our freezing completely to death. We would need lumber that we didn't have, and some nails and a saw and a claw hammer, all three of which were in a toolbox on the back porch. Our plan was simple. We would hammer together a large rectangular box, one large and deep enough to hold an impressive supply of coal. We would mount the box on four legs, two of them, the hind legs, longer than those in front, giving our box the slant necessary for the coal to go tumbling out of the box when we opened the door that we would install at the center of the lower side of the rectangle.

We drew plans and diagrams, then went about gathering the necessary lumber. It did not take very long. We found several short two-by-fours and some discarded barn boards at the village dump, then walked the local alleys until we had scrounged enough additional one-bys to flesh out our project's demands. We followed our diagrams, more or less, as we hammered our fingers no less than our ten penny nails blue. It is a wonderful thing to watch a beautiful work of art evolve, especially if the work was devised by one's own brain and is assembled by one's own hands. And the beauty is further enhanced if the work serves a practical as well as an aesthetic need.

We took turns, my brother and I, wielding the hammer. We were on our knees most of the time, our materials having been laid out on a flat, grassy area west of the tool shed. We talked as we worked, mostly observations related to the ingenuity of our project. My little brother was a very pleasant fellow worker, brown-eyed and fair-haired and spunky, and he laughed a lot, sometimes at things that weren't even funny. He wasn't much bigger than the hammer we took turns with, but he caught on quickly – "caught on" being our mother's phrase – to anything difficult enough to offer a genuine challenge.

Observe, for example, how smoothly he has fit the edge of one board against the edge of another, how securely he has nailed these boards to a two-by-four, how carefully he now is measuring the length of one of the legs I will take from him to do the sawing. We have the plans and the diagrams on a lined sheet of paper from a Big Chief tablet, but the procedure itself must be improvised, felt out, intuited – because, finally, there is no road map for genius or for where genius might find itself going.

Even so, when the project stood on its own four legs it wobbled considerably, forcing us to shorten first one of the hind legs, then one of the front legs, then the other hind one, until we wondered whether the rectangular bin sloped sufficiently to permit the coal to rush through the door, the door with its hinges and latch having caused its creators several challenging moments.

For some time we stood to one side, then another, admiring our handiwork, which had taken us most of a Saturday to finish. My little brother seemed pleased. He worked the latch, opened the door, waited a few moments while the coal that wasn't there spilled into the coal bucket; then, having closed and latched the door, he repeated the process, each time exclaiming, *Goddamn*. The truth is, my brother took enormous pleasure in his swearing, and I took enormous pleasure in my brother's pleasure. I too knew how to swear, and I too enjoyed hearing myself say those awful words I so often heard my father say, but I do not believe that the pleasure I derived from my own swearing equaled the pleasure my brother took when working the door of our immaculate project he said, *Goddamn*. And I must say also, in the interest of Truth, that neither of us could swear with a lyricism sufficiently intense or melodic to challenge our father's. We knew the words, or some of them, as Mark Twain might have put it, but we didn't know the music.

What my brother was saying with his irreverence was that the consequence of our day's work was nothing less than remarkable. And certainly I did not disagree.

But will it work?

We had no coal to do any experimenting with, and we knew that Father would not have a load delivered until the first winter storm arrived, which probably would not happen for at least two or three months. So we needed to think of something to use as a reasonable substitute.

I know, Johnny said. Let's try it with rocks!

So we walked the sides of many streets, gathering rocks and dropping them into coffee cans that our mother saved for – what? We didn't know, but we did know where to find the cans – in the cave, in the storm shelter, on an empty shelf above glimmering jars of beans and peaches.

We walked the sides of the streets because a recent shower had brought out the local road grader, and always its enormous blade would uncover rocks of all descriptions and would deliver them, with a film of moist earth, to the side of the road, sometimes all the way into the ditch. Up one street and down another we walked, filling the cans then taking them to our newly created bin where we dumped them, then back to the road until again the cans were overflowing, then . . .

We did not fill the rectangular box to its capacity, but when we figured that we had enough rocks to provide a legitimate test we placed one of the cans on the ground under the door, then stood back for a moment or two of silent evaluation. Yes, everything seemed to be in order – wooden box with one end higher than the other, rocks of various shapes and sizes filling the lower third of the bin, door latched, coffee can (Folgers, capacity two pounds plus) on the ground.

Johnny did the honors. And we watched as the rocks, a few of them, more dribbled than tumbled into the coffee can. Johnny said, *Goddamn*, this time with a somewhat different inflection.

What it meant was that our project needed some revising, some adjusting, some fine-tuning – because after only a few seconds of dribbling, the flow stopped altogether, and for the following reasons:

1) The slope, thanks to our efforts to level the legs, was not severe enough, and

2) The box needed to be more in the shape of a funnel than a rectangle to permit the coal to slide down and then out of the small end of the spout.

We made the adjustments, my brother and I, without any paper-and-pencil preplanning. Two boards placed at angles inside the bin would provide a V to guide the coal to the door, and longer hind legs would give the box a greater slope.

Creating the V was easy, but lengthening the hind legs proved troublesome. My brother measured and I sawed, then together we nailed each shorter length to each longer one. But again the creation wobbled, and after two or three additional corrections wobbled some more. Well, I said at last, shit. Then Johnny, who could easily have been an engineer, said, Let's leave the legs alone and do something to the ground.

And we did. Ever so carefully we used the family shovel to rearrange the topography of God's good earth, a divot here, a skimming of grass there, until our creation stood solid, perhaps, as a pyramid. We looked at it and Johnny nodded, grinning. He had a substantial gap between his two large upper teeth, a gap he used just now to spit through.

We gathered some more rocks, then gave our invention another try. And O the sweet, sweet sound of the rocks cascading down the slope and through the door was equaled only by the sound they made when they fell into the coffee can. When the can was full Johnny closed the door, and after we had congratulated ourselves

and had determined not to scavenge paint to paint our masterpiece we went off somewhere to do something else while awaiting
the arrival of winter.

In south-central Kansas winter almost always arrives when you
least expect it, which is one reason that Father had not ordered a
load of coal before the first snowfall. But it didn't take Andrew
Martin, the town drayman, long to come to our rescue; shortly
after Mother encouraged Father to call him, his enormous truck
eased itself down the alley, backed itself to within several yards of
our invention, raised its bed and deposited an echelon of coal high
enough to last us maybe until Christmas.

No sooner was he out of sight than Johnny and I were at work,
in spite of a north wind that threatened either to freeze us or blow
us away, or both. We could not have cared less. We took turns with
the family shovel, filling then dumping its load into the bin of our
invention, until Johnny suggested that we first fill a half-bushel
basket, then together carry it to the bin and together raise it and
dump it. His nose was running and there was water in his eyes.

When at last the bin was full we fetched the coal bucket and
placed it on the ground beneath the door which, owing to the relentless north wind and blowing snow, most of which found its
way into our benumbed faces, Johnny did not take long to open. A
few pieces of coal fell into the bucket, then a few more, but there
was no cascade. We waited. One or two pieces eased reluctantly to
the edge of the door, then just as reluctantly counted ten before
dropping over.

We stood there, my brother and I, experiencing utter disbelief,
until after a long time I picked up the family shovel and poked at
the coal until some of it slid downward, some of it finally moving
through the door, some of it finally dropping into the coal bucket.

But it became obvious that the coal was not going to do much sliding on its own, because each time I stopped the nudging the coal stopped its sliding. With arms growing weary from the weight of the family shovel I eventually decided that nudging the coal with a long-handled instrument was not, and never had been, a part of our plan.

So I tossed the shovel as if a javelin into the middle of next Wednesday.

My brother, grinning, understood. He said, I believe both gleefully and resignedly, *Goddamn*.

How far must one walk, do you suppose, to reach the middle of next Wednesday? Not very far. So I retrieved the shovel as my little brother picked up the coal bucket. We met then at the echelon of dirty fuel that Andrew Martin's truck had left us, and I filled the bucket with coal and together my brother and I carried it to the house and into the living room, where beside the old Warm Morning stove with its many little windows of isinglass and its blackened pipe – a one-armed monster reaching up and into the ceiling – we sat it down.

No more coal. Should our father's enterprise succeed, my brother and I would haul *no more coal* – not this winter, not next winter, not ever. The possibility of our never again hauling coal warmed us, consoled us, thrilled us. We could go to the failed coal bin, go to where it stood just west of the tool shed, stood with its door open and its bin half filled with coal, could go there and stand beside our failed creation and say, Piss on you, double piss on you, and if it were night we could do it, could pull out our little peckers and piss on it and feel so good it would make us shiver, even though it might still be summer.

When hope grows strong enough, it moves beyond possibility

into certainty. Bucket by bucket I carried dirt from the cave up the steps and out of the porch and across the driveway to dump it on a mound whose enormity, in the eyes of a boy, offered further hope. Surely so much dirt must mean eventual success. Patience. One bucket at a time. And the passageway, its sides so cleanly beveled, moves south, then bucket by bucket turns east, and there is music in the turning, music quietly vibrant in the echo chamber of the tunnel, *What a beautiful thought I am thinking, concerning the great speckled bird*, and the anger and the spite are gone from the father's eyes, *I'm saving up coupons to buy one of those*, and Mother seems happier, too, and my sister also, who Mother says is about to become a woman, and Christ on a crutch Christmas is coming, and when it arrives we will have a new floor furnace and the old Warm Morning stove will be gone forever and forever, will it not?

3

On the off-chance that one of these days I'll die, I ask only that you boys see to it that I'm buried in my Chevrolet.

—Clarence Bingham, 1932–1984

The strongest of all warriors are these two – Time and Patience.

—Leo Tolstoy, *War and Peace*

The aborigines of New Zealand are called Maoris, a Polynesian people. . . . Among them, it was supposed that the seat of the soul was the left eye.

—*Lincoln Library of Essential Information*

Here's how you do it: You drive your Chevy, the black one you'll put everything you own into this fall when you leave for college, and with two buddies, Jimmy and Carl, you head west on the highway to that place where the macadam doglegs left for several hundred feet before it doglegs right, and near the center of those several hundred feet is where the railroad crosses, so of course that is where you maneuver the Chevy until you have its tires on the tracks, tires underinflated so they'll settle softly onto the tracks when you continue west, now not on the highway but on the tracks that parallel the highway, Jimmy in the front seat at your right, Carl in the back seat behind him, Jimmy that likable bag of wind telling you again, then again, not to touch the steering wheel, don't even breathe heavily on it, he says likably, his smile a mile wide, just let the car do its own steering, which if you keep your hands and your breath off the wheel it will, the underinflated tires providing cushions to keep the Chevy on the tracks, and here you go, you and Jimmy that likable bag of wind and Carl, who is so quiet and devoid of expression he's inscrutable, here you go, heading west toward Sharon where you intend to turn around and head back east, giving your Chevy its rein, its windows rolled down, one of your arms with a hand at its end waving to whatever asks or doesn't ask to be waved at, birds and horses and cows and trees and clouds and humans who in their inferior vehicles traveling on the inferior road that runs parallel to the tracks wave back, they being probably both amazed and envious, and holy cow you haven't had this much fun since Hector was a pup, since somebody's mother, but not your own, caught a tit in the wringer of the Maytag washer. That's how you do it, all right. In five years, give or take, that's how you'll do it.

Meanwhile, the passageway under our house was evolving into nothing short of a masterpiece, partly because my father took such pains to bevel its sides, and partly because by the end of October it was almost finished. Patience. If the dog continues to place one leg over the other he will arrive in Dover. Rome wasn't built in a day, Mother told us each time we showed so much as a trace of discouragement, and though I appreciated the sentiment I really didn't give one hoot in Halifax about Rome, wherever it might be or whenever it might have been finished.

One late afternoon as we were preparing to remove some additional dirt, Father told me to fetch him the longest nail I could find, so I went directly to the nail box in the tool shed, emptied its contents on the floor and began to rummage. Our nail box was perhaps misnamed. It was not a box, but a large can, and it contained not only nails but also nuts and bolts and screws and small hinges and maybe a dead bug or two. Even so, we called it the nail box, probably because in the beginning we had intended it to be exclusively a nail box. But somehow nuts and bolts and so forth found their way into the can, so that when we needed anything smaller than a John Deere tractor we went to the nail box fully intending to find it.

I selected the largest nail and because I believed that my father was in a hurry I did not return the scattered contents to the can.

I found my father in the house waiting for me, a hammer in his right hand. I gave him the nail, which he looked at approvingly. Then together we walked to that line where the living room and the dining room joined, and there, after two or three rather nonscientific measurements, Father drove the nail into the pine floor to mark the center of that place where he intended to locate the furnace.

Back under the house then, in the tunnel, Father manipulated

48

the light until he saw among a network of smaller nail-points the larger nail, and then I saw it too, and I was delighted that it was not far from where the tunnel ended, and I believe that my father was equally delighted. He grinned. Not a trace of spite in his grass-green eyes, not a trace of anger. And I tried to remember: Had there ever been?

When our digging of the passageway took us to a point directly under the nail, and after Father had beveled the sides to his satisfaction, we began the task of clearing a space large enough to accommodate the furnace. I had no idea how large this space should be, of course, but it turned out to be much larger than I had guessed. It seemed to me that Father, having begun the widening and the deepening of the end of the tunnel, might not stop until he had made space enough for half a dozen furnaces, but I had carried too many cans and buckets of dirt up the earthen stairs and out of the porch and across the driveway to dump on a hill that had become a mountain to lodge a complaint. Once in a while my subaltern, Johnny, would say something soft but unkind under his breath, something with which I did not disagree. But I pretty much kept my mouth shut. I knew that Johnny's occasional utterances were more smoke than fire. I knew that deep in his heart my brother was less defiant than anxious. No more coal. No more *goddamn* coal. Doggedly, we traded an empty container for one that was full, or half full, and proceeded on.

Until you turn your head to say something to Carl, and you turn the head too far so that the torso moves with it, and the left arm moves with the torso, and the left wrist strikes the steering wheel and the Chevy veers to the right, jumping the tracks, and Jimmy that sweet sack of shit says O shit and Carl doesn't say anything and the vehicle is bumping over the ties and the chat like the runaway stagecoach

you watched the other night at the Rialto and before you can clutch
and move the gearshift into neutral the car has stopped and the mo-
tor has died and there you are in the middle of nowhere unable to
wish that Ray Wilson with his uncanny strength were here to lift the
Chevy back onto the tracks, or to heave it over the rails and onto the
right-of-way, because at the moment you don't know squat about
railroading because you'll not be a gandy dancer until next summer
but the green board you're seeing to the west was red a moment ago
and the change from red to green must surely mean something, prob-
ably that a train is approaching, and all you can do is sit there behind
the wheel like a lump on a sinking log and pray for something beyond
what you understand as human to deliver you.

When the space at last was cleared, and the lard can and the calf
bucket hung on nails in the tool shed, Johnny and I were left with
little to do but wait for someone else to do something. And someone else did. He was the local handyman, Philip Payne, and by the
middle of November he had installed the furnace and had hooked
this wire to that one, had screwed this gas pipe to another and had
sawed a large rectangular hole in the floor at that place where the
large nail had been driven and had covered the hole with a grate
and had wiped his hands on his overalls before giving my father a
piece of paper that said how much we owed him.

I doubt that we owed him very much, because Mother had a
talent for swapping good hot meals for services rendered, and Mr.
Payne liked good hot meals, and he liked my mother, too, as did
everyone in town except much of the time my father, so I am
speculating that the bill, whatever it was, was – in the context of
the times and circumstances – minimal.

But anyway, who cared? The project had been completed, and
each member of the family had contributed – Mother by goading

Father into undertaking the project, Father by accepting and finishing it – his tunnel beautifully and amply sculpted – sister by working overtime at the cafe, sons by toting away uncountable buckets and cans of south-central Kansas dirt. We were a family, after all, by God, and by God come the first cold snap we would be a warm and cozy family, a family not without its comforts, notwithstanding the absence of an indoor facility and something softer than a rock or a brick for my sister to sleep on.

You tell the others that the board ahead has changed from red to green and maybe that means something, maybe a train approaching, and Jimmy says O shit and the other breaks his silence to suggest that you try starting the car – and the car because you are praying starts, and in low gear, with Jimmy and Carl at the rear pushing and lifting and grunting like Neanderthals, you move the prewar vehicle over the ties one at a time, smoke from under the car coming from somewhere, one tie at a time, and you can see that ahead, maybe fifty yards ahead, roughly half the length of the field last fall you defeated the Harper Bearcats on, there is thank you Jesus a road crossing, so that crossing becomes the goal line, pay dirt, reach the end zone boys and you can celebrate, the light ahead no longer red but green, greener even than your father's eyes, so as you work the clutch and the footfeed to cajole the car over the ties one by one you look frequently in the rearview mirror, hoping not to see the eye of a monster growing larger behind you, smoke both white and blue rising from beneath the black Chevy that you bought with your own money, thanks to a summer job that paid handsomely, paid enough for you to buy the car and have enough left over for tuition and maybe room and board, and at the moment you see no eye of a monster in the rearview mirror, the crossing ahead coming closer, but very slowly, Jimmy and Carl with their strong young backs pushing and

lifting and grunting, you working the clutch and the footfeed, the car
bouncing up and over and down one tie, then another, one tie at a
time, the Chevy smoking more heavily now and one tie at a time you
pass the steel pole at the top of which the green light glows and you
look in the rearview mirror again and you believe you see something
well behind you on the tracks and you work the clutch and the foot-
feed with additional zeal, the Chevy continuing to respond, but not
until the clutch has been almost totally released, the boys at the rear
pushing and lifting and grunting in a rhythm that under less omi-
nous circumstances might have suggested music.

When the first cold snap arrived, and we clicked on the furnace, and the furnace clicked back and sent warm air up and out of the register, and the living and dining rooms became quickly comfortable without the odor of coal, we clapped like a satisfied congregation – or would have clapped, had we all been together, which we weren't, Father and Mother having left early for the cafe, and their children, one child at a time, having arisen to prepare for school.

And to this day I believe that it was the advent of the floor furnace that introduced me to the wonders of a formal education, because the furnace not only warmed our bodies but it likewise warmed my mother's heart – warmed it, that is, to a degree so exceptional that when a salesman one day in late November materialized on the front porch my mother not only invited him in, she also listened to him and believed him and for a sum of money not yet disclosed she bought his product, a thick reference book with gold lettering on its green cover: *The Lincoln Library of Essential Information.*

Jesus and boy howdy. Father was not altogether pleased, but he shook his head and mumbled a few words, perhaps expletives, and we children made a circle around the book and took turns holding it and smelling it and turning its veritable millions of pages. We had never seen a book both so new and so large, and it was ours, our very own, our very own library – The cover called it a library, so who could argue? – contained in a single volume. Did Mother buy the book because the room she bought it in was being heated not by a smelly Warm Morning coal stove but by a furnace installed, more or less, by Ralph, her husband? Surely that had been a reason, however major or minor. Another might have been that the cafe was providing the family a decent income, probably because my parents and their hired cook, Edna Hatfield, kept the place open from sunup until ten or eleven at night. But a third factor must have been significant if not dominant: She wanted her children to have a solid education, and she wanted to express this desire with something impressively thick and tangible, something for which her children might praise her when they became well-educated and highly successful. True, the school had a library, a small one, but there was no public library, and in any case there was no substitute for a family's having its own library, especially if this library were complete in one volume and had been purchased by a mother who very sincerely wanted her children to make something of themselves, and to do this by using their heads for something far more than hat racks.

Mother had graduated from high school, from the same school that her children now were attending. She had married a man with a strong back who had not gone to high school, and thus had no diploma, because he and his strong back were needed to help with farm work on his father's quarter section of mediocre soil in south-central Kansas. My father's story was an old one. His father had been one of many children that his German father had not been able to afford, so Grandfather left home and took to farming at an early age. No matter the size of the acreage, or the difficulties that its meagerness entailed, he considered himself lucky to be no longer under the dictatorial thumb of his father. My father, in turn, left home as soon as an opportunity presented itself; he did not want to exist under the dictatorial thumb of his father, and he foresaw, probably correctly, that his father's acreage would never yield more crops than headaches. So he left, counting himself lucky to have escaped his one-cow environment, regardless of what he might find himself doing thereafter.

This is the man, then, that my mother married, and because she was a woman with an easy laugh and a sharp eye who always wanted to better herself, her choice of a mate must have been prompted more by passion than logic. Or perhaps she, too, wanted to leave home at an early age (she married at nineteen), her widowed mother a short wide ornery German immigrant who as a grandmother I loved and detested in large and equal amounts. So Mother might have taken Father as a convenient means of escape, perhaps believing that in spite of his constricted education he might somehow fall into a position that surely as a young strapping fellow he deserved — and she, as his wife, would harvest her equal share of the benefits.

This did not happen. My father bounced like an ill-devised rubber ball from one back-breaking job to another. Ironically, one of the first was that of farmer. From a man named Broce he rented a few acres north of town, and for almost three years he plowed and planted and milked two or three cows and raised two or three hogs and endured a confederation of chickens until two years after my birth Mr. Broce decided that he no longer wanted to rent the farm, he wanted to run it, so my father bought one of the cows and one of the hogs and he and Mother packed our worldly goods into whatever it was we called a motor vehicle and we moved into town. Then as a harvest hand he was out of bed before the chickens greasing the zerks on someone else's combine so that the machine might run smoothly as he inhaled chaff and scooped the wheat he'd drive then to the elevator. As a common laborer for the county, Harper County, he repaired bridges and patched roads until a floating kidney and a double hernia and the loss of two fingers forced him to take the position of *road maintainer*, which meant that the position was an upright one, my father standing behind the wheel of a road grader that shook and shimmied from dawn until sunset, my father shaking and shimmying with it as with one hand he held the wheel steady while with the other hand, the one with two fingers missing, he worked the levers to adjust the almighty blade.

During these many years my mother laughed easily and never lost the sharpness in her eyes. During all these years she must have believed that, sooner or later, some reputable, decent-paying job would find them, or they would find it, and the family would enjoy the prosperity it deserved.

No, that image in the rearview mirror is not the face of a locomotive; it must have been a vehicle crossing the tracks, or maybe a mirage prompted by the urgency of the moment, and you check the mirror again to be certain, then you blink your eyes rapidly to clear them and with clear eyes you judge that the crossing ahead cannot be more than fifteen yards away, one first-and-ten plus five, so you grimace and to make certain that the grimace is sufficiently grim you check it in the rearview mirror where at its lower edge you can see Jimmy and Carl lifting and pushing, Jimmy's likable cheeks filled with a portion of his inexhaustible supply of hot air, he having been the one to suggest that you try this adventure, he never having done it before but he knew it would work, he had measured the width of both tracks and several cars, Carl's face appropriately resolute, Carl the farm boy who

drives his parents' station wagon as if he owns it, his parents like
yours not getting along very well, so on Saturday nights you ride with
him in the station wagon, ride and talk until midnight, then ride and
talk some more, and this time when you check the rearview mirror
what you see by God is neither a distant vehicle crossing the tracks
nor a mirage but smoke rising from the stack of an unmistakable
locomotive and you work the clutch and the footfeed to take the
Chevy over yet another tie and there is no response, the clutch sure
enough having burned completely out, not much smoke now coming
from the underside of the car, and leaving the gear shift in neutral
you jump out and shut the door and standing beside the car, one
hand through the open window on the wheel, you add your own
weight and thrust to that being provided by your buddies and the
black Chevy responds and you arrive at the crossing barely in time to
turn the car off the tracks before the train, a freight, sends its dark
deadly shadow swiftly over you, over you and your buddies and your
car, and you blink your eyes and hold your hands over your ears until
the locomotive with its whistle and its thick rope of smoke swirls past
and you don't move as the train cars swaying slightly and heavily
clickety-clack the rails and you look at that place where one of the
rails joins the other, both held firmly in line by iron bars, and when
the caboose passes and the man aboard smiles and waves, well you'll
be damned if you don't smile and wave too.

My mother's optimism perhaps prompted her to be, at least at
times, something between a nag and a scold. She no doubt saw
herself as one whose cheerleading was necessary if the family ever
hoped to better itself. And the bettering would not occur, not ever,
if she did not almost daily prod my father. There is an enormous
difference between You *must* do it and You *can* do it. It is the yawn-

ing chasm between mandate and encouragement. I am guessing that for my mother this chasm was frequently little more than a hairline fissure.

So my father, sufficiently bolstered, one day stopped working for others and started working for himself. He bought a service station, a filling station, and though it was the smallest station in town it nonetheless attracted a modest number of loyal customers, plus some strangers driving east or west along Highway 160, those who needed gas or oil and did not care to turn south and find a different station at the far end of the main street. It was a business comfortable in its smallness, or so it seemed to me, and unlike the other stations, the Mobil and the Champlin, it did not have a mechanic on duty, and that absence of a mechanic most certainly included my father. His method of healing an ailing vehicle was to look it squarely in the eyes and swear at it, soundly and thoroughly. Of course he used this method chiefly on his own automobile, and for the most part it worked. That is, he would swear at the beast until someone heard him and came to his aid, someone who owned a comprehensive set of tools and who knew a dome light from a camshaft. Always, it seemed, such a person would be out there, toolbox in hand, waiting for some lost soul to call, and that person would respond, would bloody his knuckles while dirtying himself from cap to boots until the job was finished, and more times than not he would refuse payment, and my father, his anger ancient history, would thank him and shake his greasy hand and tell him to drop by the station, if at that moment he still owned the station, and he'd treat him to a free change of oil.

One lazy summer day I was inside the station, tending to business because my father had gone uptown to lunch, when a young boy walked through the door and asked where I kept the candy. I showed him – right here, I said, on the counter, and I led him to where our supply of candy rested on a display shelf atop the counter. The boy could scarcely see over the counter, but he managed. It was not a large supply – an assortment of gums, Juicy Fruit and Doublemint and Spearmint and Blackjack and Yucatan, some small packages of peanuts, a few little boxes of redhots, maybe a twist or two of licorice.

And one thin shiny packet of something I could not identify. Because confession is good for the soul, or so they say, I'll confess: I had found the small shiny package while in the act of snooping, an act that I had begun shortly after my father headed uptown for lunch. He had left me in charge because he knew that for the most part his customers could help themselves, and he trusted me, and everyone else, not to tinker with what little money there might be in the cash register. Business had been slow, and to relieve the tedium I explored the nooks and the crannies of our little station, the most interesting being the long shelf under the counter. Odds and ends had found their way onto the shelf, and because light from the overhead bulb was partially obscured by the counter these odds and ends took on a shadowy significance. For example, one day I found a box of used zerks, each of them, I suppose, cheap enough to throw away but nice enough to keep. At the time I did not know what they were. So I showed them to my father, who called them zerks and told me how they worked; he went so far as to affix one of them to the end of a grease gun, whereupon he pumped grease through the zerk, a fitting that attached to a vehicle would have delivered grease to whatever needed greasing. On another occasion I discovered a square board with some small holes in it, a board that looked new, like a game that had not been played very often. That's a punchboard, Father said, and I want you to leave it the hell alone. I did not ask anything further. I put the punchboard back in its place, where I left it the hell alone.

But the small packets were another matter; they intrigued me beyond my ability to leave them alone. There were many of them in a cardboard box, all very neatly and compactly packaged, and each was shiny as a new dime in its wrapping of cellophane. I removed one from the box and felt its smoothness between a thumb and an index finger. At the time I knew very little about the fine art of marketing, but I knew that the little packet was pleasing to both eye and touch, and I concluded that such an appealing item should not be withheld from potential customers. So I had placed the shiny little package on the shelf with the candy, next to the Blackjack gum.

The youngster stood for a long time weighing his options. His right hand was a fist containing coins that he would give me when he made his decisions, which he did not make until he had touched each item, excluding the redhots, several times. At last he decided upon one package of Juicy Fruit gum and the small shiny packet that I had so recently put on display. I did not know what to charge him for this item of mystery, so I took all of his change, two pennies, I believe, and a nickel, and told him, You're welcome when he told me, Thank you, and he walked away rubbing the shiny cellophane and whatever it contained between a thumb and an index finger.

When Father returned from lunch I told him what had happened. He frowned, to begin with, then the frown turned to a smile and the smile moved into laughter and I couldn't help myself – I laughed also, because my father did not laugh like that very often, and it was funny to see him laughing, and I wanted to be a part of his fun. When he was finished he said, Condom. O Christ!

That boy bought a condom. Then he told me it was all right this time, but hereafter I was to leave the condoms the hell alone, which until I learned what the hell a condom was I did.

It is Carl who hitchhikes back into town where he goes straight to the station wagon, then straight to the Mobil station for a length of chain, then returns to where you and Jimmy are standing on a gravel road beside a clutchless black Chevy, Jimmy laughing at what has happened, you laughing too, though maybe not as hard as Jimmy, it being your car that now sits on the gravel road, clutchless, and you wonder how much it will cost to replace the clutch, wonder if Hadsall at the Champlin station can do the work, how long it will take, what your father will say, your mother, wonder why you listened to Jimmy in the first place, the goddamn windbag, but likable, and anyhow it was fun, wasn't it, sailing along on the tracks with your arm out the window like the wing of a bird, the Chevy like the bird's huge unlikely body, folks in their cars on the highway waving at you and your wing waving back, and you help Carl attach the chain to pull you into town, Jimmy beside you laughing and talking and breaking into song, maybe a hymn, he has such a high sweet voice and he wants to be a missionary, and because you know the words to the hymn you sing along, the chain between the Chevy and the station wagon keeping you connected and moving – because Carl has such a heavy foot – much too rapidly along.

It took only a week or so for my sister to lose interest in *The Lincoln Library of Essential Information*. She had seen it and held it and had turned some of its pages, perhaps had read a couple of its sentences, and that was enough. She was at the edge of becoming a woman, Mother said, and that maybe explained it. And Johnny – well, the book was not as tall as my brother, and not quite as wide, but surely it almost outweighed him, so like my sister he deferred to me, and thus I became the undisputed keeper of the family's one-volume library.

For a while I kept it on top of an upright orange crate beside my bed, on a white doily crocheted by my German grandmother. Beneath it, on the shelf provided by the partition at the center of the crate, rested several comic books – *The Torch and Toro, Captain Marvel, Batman and Robin, The Green Lantern.* These were wonderful books, and I did not neglect them. Almost every night I'd read one or two, my little brother beside me reading also, a box of soda crackers between us, something to drink, juice or milk, on Grandmother's doily atop the orange crate. But when I placed the *Lincoln Library* atop the doily, I had no platform on which to rest our libations, except on the book's green cover; so before long I lugged the book into the dining room and found a place for it on the table near the buffet where Father kept his coupons. It was an ideal location, plenty of space to open the book and turn its uncountable pages, to gather information that according to the gold lettering on the green cover was essential.

It is essential to know that Alabama's state bird is the yellowhammer, essential to learn that Attila the Hun was no less a windbag than my buddy Jimmy would be, Attila boasting that grass never grew again where his gallant horse's hooves had trod.

On a blustery winter evening, our floor furnace purring like a large, mysterious, domesticated animal, I'd stand at the table discovering information that is indeed essential – and, by virtue of what was excluded, is not. Do you know that if a horsehair is thrown into a pool, the hair will be changed into a snake? That's what many people, long ago, believed, and what some people living today still do. Boy howdy.

It was a special time, that winter of the new floor furnace. My brother and I had carried away the dirt that helped to make the warm air from the furnace possible (which meant that we no more were required to carry buckets of black dusty coal halfway across the continent and into the house to feed a Warm Morning's insatiable appetite), which in turn had lifted my mother's spirits – and my father's also – and my sister was becoming a young woman and Christmas, Mother said, was just around the corner, and the memory of Father dismantling the old coal-burner for me to carry piece by heavy piece to the family junk pile at the edge of the alley between the barn and the outhouse provided additional warmth, and this: In 1870, seven thousand buildings in Istanbul, which is in Turkey, burned to the ground at an estimated loss of twenty-five million dollars.

Yes, Hadsall can do the job for you, he'll have to send to Harper for a new clutch, and the cost will certainly diminish but not deplete your bank account, the one you took such pride in when you established it around the middle of May, signed over your initial pay-check to a certified fartknocker who once upon a time denied your father a small loan because he didn't have half a million dollars in collateral, but it's the only bank in town, and shitfire one banker is like all the rest, your father says, all of them together not worth the cost of the dynamite it would take to blow their fucking brains out, so you sign not only your own check but a couple of official looking papers and you walk out the door with a bank account, money enough by the end of the summer to buy yourself a car, an old '38 Chevy, as it turns out, with enough money left over for books and tuition and, as it turns out, a new clutch, your father having very nearly grinned when you told him what had happened, your mother's anger and disappointment overwhelmed by relief and gratefulness, you anxious as a child with the heebie-jeebies as you wait for Hadsall to send for the new clutch and install it, your buddy Carl anxious too, the two of you cruising the streets of a town you say you can't wait to escape from, Carl, one year older than you, not certain where to go or what to do with his farm-boy life, you about to head to a campus you know practically nothing about, you and Carl in his pale blue station wagon cruising and talking, both sets of parents coming uninvited into the conversation, both sets adrift in similar boats they cannot or will not stop rocking, and though it isn't Saturday night the main street is active, business good in the Rexall drugstore and the pool hall and my parents' cafe, and sooner or later you replay that near miss on the railroad tracks, telling each other more than once that except for someone touching the goddamn steering wheel that's how you do it, all right, that's exactly how you do it.

One problem with the one-volume library is that no matter how thick it is, it is never quite thick enough.

I learned this lesson when for some unaccountable reason I could not remember the real names of Batman and Robin. So I went to the *Lincoln Library*'s index where, no matter how closely I looked, I could find no information whatsoever related to my heroes. I was stunned – until it occurred to me that no book is perfect, that the editors had overlooked this essential information and that as a boy doing his best to follow the Golden Rule I should forgive them. So I did. But my compassion did not last very long, because when I tried to find other essential information – the name of the boy who by shouting *Shazam!* could transform himself into Captain Marvel, or the name of the people from whom Wonder Woman descended – I drew additional blanks. Clearly, something was amiss. Clearly, the editors of my one-volume library either had deliberately misled me with its title, or could not always distinguish the essential from the non-essential. I knew absolutely that the street names of Batman and Robin – Bruce Wayne and Dick Grayson – were essential, knew absolutely that if one did not recognize the name Billy Batson or did not know that Wonder Woman's people were the Amazonians, one's education was woefully deficient – whereupon I compiled a list of my own essentials, and none of them, including the fact that some pinball machines tilt more readily than others, was in the *Lincoln Library*'s index.

My first impulse was to throw my one-volume library into the trash. But I didn't. It had taught me a truth more significant than revenge – that experts who did not grow up in drugstores and pool halls and barber shops and filling stations deserve pity more than scorn. They probably had not read either the Sears and Roebuck or Montgomery Ward catalogs, and it would not have surprised me if they had not memorized verses of Scripture, and thus did not know, as did Amos, that woe is in store for those unfortunate creatures who lie upon beds of ivory.

It is a good thing to know that experts do not know everything. Knowing this, I kept my one-volume library and smiled and shook my head each time I discovered yet another omission. And another cold snap occurred, then another, and the floor furnace kept pace, warming the living room and the dining room and removing some of the chill from the kitchen and the bedrooms. Two or three times during that winter I ventured onto the back porch to lift the door to the cave, then carefully descended the earthen stairs to wander the earthen floor with a hand raised until I found the string that, pulled, would switch on the light. And I would stand there looking at the passageway that in a minute or so I would follow to where the furnace sat in its ample space, purring. With the family shovel Father had beveled the sides of that space, and the sides of the tunnel, and with a calf bucket and a lard container my brother and I had carried the dirt across the floor and up the earthen steps and out the door and across the gravel driveway to dump it on a patch of bunchgrass just east of the outhouse. Dirt. And patience. And one leg over the other the dog walks to Dover. And when the mound rose halfway to the height of the outhouse my little brother stood atop it, claiming to be King of the Mountain – until his older brother with the full force of an entire Mongolian horde ascended the mountain and executing a flanking movement kicked the ass of his feisty but smaller brother squarely into the middle of next Wednesday, Father meanwhile whistling, or singing, the only lines he knew from "The Great Speckled Bird."

4

And what is education but the process of expanding the individual consciousness to include as much of race consciousness as possible, with universal sympathy as the ideal achievement?

—John Neihardt, *All Is but a Beginning*

Training is everything. The peach was once a bitter almond; cauli-flower is nothing but cabbage with a college education.

—Mark Twain, *Pudd'nhead Wilson*

I, too, dislike it: there are things that are important beyond all this
  fiddle.
 Reading it, however, with a perfect contempt for it, one discovers
  that there is in
 it after all, a place for the genuine.

—Marianne Moore, "Poetry"

Two blocks east of the teachers college campus I rented a second-story sunroom that I shared with two high-school buddies, Toar Grant and Gene Carpenter. We each paid twelve dollars a month for a bed, a desk with a chair, and a portable closet in which to store and hang our clothes. It was a cozy room, half a dozen windows across the west side, a single window on the north side, and another on the south. Four additional rooms were on this same floor, all of them occupied by students, most of them upperclassmen, all of us sharing one small bathroom.

I was perhaps the greenest freshman ever to have enrolled in a college or university. I had corresponded with the office of admissions to the extent that I knew where and when to appear to meet with my adviser to enroll, and that was it. I had not bothered to peruse the college catalog; I do not remember receiving a catalog, though probably I had – and probably I had viewed it as unreasonably complex and had tossed it away. I was attending this teachers college because my friend Toar Grant had told me about it, and Toar knew at least the name and location of the college because his uncle Bernard had distinguished himself there as a quarter-miler.

Though I knew next to nothing about the process of enrolling in college, I was not altogether an ignoramus. I knew the street names of Batman and Robin, didn't I? I knew, from having studied the colorful pages of the Sears and Roebuck catalog, the meaning of comparatives and superlatives: This shirt is *good*, this one *better*, this one *best*. Because I had been active in the boy scouts and had climbed my way up the ladder from Tenderfoot to Eagle, I knew a square knot from a granny, knew the seven pressure points, knew how to box the compass, how to start a fire with tinder and flint (and, having failed, with matches), how to build and employ a reflector oven. From the *Lincoln Library* I was aware of Attila the Hun's notoriety, but the book neglected to inform me that on his wedding night he died from a nosebleed. Thus I learned that my one-volume library was not inclusive in more ways than one. And from the Scriptures I had gleaned a multitude of sometimes contradictory admonitions and declarations and, as in the case of one's inviting woe should one sleep on a bed of ivory, confusions.

And I was familiar with half a dozen poems, two of which I cannot erase from memory.

Both were included in a group that as a high-school junior I had chosen to work with as I prepared to enter the regional speech competition in Pratt. I had no interest whatsoever in poetry more refined than limericks and bathroom ditties, but some of my classmates had committed themselves to the competition and I followed along; and, too, the festival would take place on a Friday, a school day, and it would be held in a city much larger than my village of seven hundred. I could not resist.

So I chose a category labeled Oral Interpretation: Poetry. My English teacher, an elderly woman with blue hair and a wide smile that suggested both warmth and false teeth, explained the rules: I must be prepared to read any one of the poems from a group of six. I would not know which of the poems I'd be required to read until I arrived at the room where I would do the reading, at which time I would be handed one of the poems.

My teacher, Mrs. Molly Cloud Houston, seemed unduly pleased that I had tossed my hat into the Oral Interpretation: Poetry ring. Probably she was surprised that a male, a dedicated jock who as left end on the Bulldog football team had a passion for smacking his helmet into the solar plexis of others who had a passion for returning the favor, would volunteer to read – of all unlikely genres – poetry. But I did – and, as it so happened, I was the only one in her class to choose this category; the others had preferred to go with prose. I remember how widely Mrs. Houston beamed when she handed me copies of the six poems. She had not been a young woman for a long, long time, yet her face, round and chubby, with bright blue eyes, gave her a childlike aspect I found almost genuinely appealing.

At home in my bedroom I read the poems again and again, practiced reading them aloud until I felt certain that no matter which title I'd be given I would come away with a superior rating. Then each day in class Mrs. Houston would call upon one or more of the contestants to come to the front of the class and read, whereupon she would smile widely and nod and once in a while offer a suggestion that she thought might improve the presentation.

I was not required to memorize the poems, but I was expected to be very, very familiar with them, familiar to the extent that I could spend a good deal of my time making eye contact with someone in the audience. O how Mrs. Molly Cloud Houston loved the phrase *eye contact*. Make *eye contact* with someone in the audience, she said again and again, *eye contact*, as she spoke it, being perhaps the connotative equivalent of something both necessary and intimate.

I found this difficult to do. Look into the eyes of Donna Grace Davis while reading poetry? Into the eyes of Ruth Crocker, who giggled at anything uttered by any member of the opposite sex if that member were looking directly at her? At Ray Asper, who knew most, maybe all, of my most closely guarded secrets – and who, at an early age, would take them with him to the grave? And it is important also, said Mrs. Houston, not to make *eye contact* with the same person each time you look up from the text. Do this, she said, and the lone individual at whom you are making *eye contact* will take the poem personally, and maybe you along with it, while others in the audience might feel slighted or neglected.

At times I almost regretted having entered the competition. But I gritted my nonpoetic teeth and endured, and time – that river whose middle name is *inexorable* – moved on, and one fine midmorning in April I found myself in the metropolis of Pratt, Kansas, standing behind a podium in a well-lighted high school classroom, my right hand holding a copy of Vachel Lindsay's "Abraham Lincoln Walks at Midnight." My judge, a handsome middle-aged woman who carried herself like you would expect the judge of Oral Interpretation: Poetry to carry herself, had handed me an envelope containing the poem, and when my name was called I had the poem out of the envelope and in my somewhat moist hand. I was ready.

Lindsay's poem was perhaps the most difficult of the six I had been rehearsing. It begins like this:

It is portentous, and a thing of state
That here at midnight, in our little town
A mourning figure walks, and will not rest,
Near the old court-house, pacing up and down.

This is a long sentence, and Mrs. Houston had advised me either to take a deep breath before moving into it, a breath deep enough to carry me to the end of the sentence, or to determine where along the way I might want to pause for air. At length, after reading the sentence many times one way, then the other, I chose to take breaths at each of the four commas. But a larger problem was that of pronouncing "portentous" not only correctly, but also naturally, as if it were a word I used frequently. The truth, of course, is that I had never used the word or heard or seen it on the page. I didn't even know what it meant. So Molly Cloud Houston, smiling widely, offered me her expertise. She pronounced the word for me, slowly, and slowly I repeated the sounds, after which she told me that the word in the context of Lindsay's poem probably means "solemn," and it occurred to me that Mr. Lindsay could have helped me considerably had he written "solemn" instead of "portentous," but it was too late now, the poet having died long before I was born, so I swallowed my disappointment and said "portentous" and took short breaths at each of the four commas, which helped me give the poem a proper pacing, Mrs. Houston said, neither too slow nor too fast, and I moved on to the tackling of other problems.

Lindsay was writing about the spirit of President Lincoln haunting his "little town" of Springfield, Illinois; the President cannot rest easy because men continue to wage war and in the interest of greed and power destroy their fellow men. The voice in the poem is that of one of the townspeople who seems to be very much aware of the president's lingering, almost brooding, presence, and from time to time this voice uses phrases that I found difficult to pronounce. One of them is a description of Mr. Lincoln: "the quaint great figure that men love." I had trouble with "quaint great figure." Mrs. Houston told me to pronounce each word forcefully, and especially to pronounce – crisply – the *t*'s at the end of "quaint" and "great." This also took some practice, as did two subsequent phrases, "dreadnaughts scouring every main" and "carries on his shawl-wrapped shoulders now." Mrs. Houston, smiling widely, had listened to me speak these phrases until "dreadnaughts" no less than "portentous" became inevitable if not entirely welcome additions to my lexicon.

Throughout the rehearsals Mrs. Houston had been very helpful. She told me, and the class, some of the history that provoked the poem – unrest in Europe, the rise of Nicholas the Second in Russia and one of the Georges in England and Kaiser Wilhelm in Germany – and the date it had been written, August of 1914. She introduced us to the niceties of iambic pentameter and of end rhyme, both of which, she said, offered a challenge to the reader because it would be tempting to present the poem as a metrical ditty, she said, and that would detract from the poem's inherent seriousness, or solemnity; and to illustrate and dramatize her point she read several of the lines metrically, exaggerating the stresses and pausing at the ends of run-on lines. When she finished, she smiled widely, and the class smiled with her, then all of us erupted into laughter.

I had paid strict attention to what Molly Cloud Houston said, even to those observations I did not fully understand. So when the days preceding the speech festival had passed, days with their sometimes interminable hours and minutes and seconds, I was ready.

I stood behind the lectern, which was thin and whose top slanted downward toward me, Vachel Lindsay's poem in my right hand, but most of it lying on the top of the lectern, my left hand at my side. I stood upright but, as instructed, not unduly rigid. There was no microphone. The room was not large and, by listening to several other contestants, students from across the region, I knew that the acoustics were excellent. And, too, I had a voice that hovered somewhere between bass and baritone.

Several of the folding chairs had been removed from the center of the room, and in this clearing on a large wooden throne sat the judge studying a clipboard. When she looked up I made *eye contact*. Then I began to read.

I was surprised that I was not very nervous, which gave me confidence. The audience was small, comprised mostly of contestants and a sprinkling of others – friends of the readers, probably, and two or three teachers, including Mrs. Houston. I fell rather quickly into the pattern that had evolved as I practiced reading the poem in front of my classmates. Clearly and distinctly I spoke the title and identified the author. I moved through the opening lines, including *portentous*, without a hitch, pausing for breath at each of the four commas. I felt myself transported in time; I was now the townsman in Springfield, Illinois, who as the voice in the poem was protesting tyranny by way of exalting President Lincoln, that

> quaint great figure that men love,
> The prairie-lawyer, master of us all.

I made *eye contact* frequently, or tried to, and certainly that included efforts to look squarely at the judge, who sat upright on her throne. She was quite professional. She looked as squarely at me as I at her, and I could see that with a pencil in her right hand she was taking notes on a pad held by the clip on her clipboard. I was careful not to stress the iambic pattern or the rhyme, not to present the poem as a metrical ditty, as Mrs. Houston had phrased it; I did not want to undercut the poem's inherent solemnity.

> The sins of all the war-lords burn his heart.
> He sees the dreadnaughts scouring every main.
> He carries on his shawl-wrapped shoulders now
> The bitterness, the folly and the pain.

Mrs. Houston had told me, and the class, that the next-to-the-last stanza, the one following "The bitterness, the folly and the pain," is the most explicitly political; it was the stanza she had focused upon when she talked about the rise of Nicholas the Second in Russia and one of the Georges in England and Kaiser Wilhelm in Germany. She knew a good deal about the political uprisings of the early twentieth century, she said, and she wanted all of us to know something about them also so that as both readers and listeners we might appreciate more fully Mr. Lindsay's passionate plea for peace and freedom.

> He cannot rest until a spirit-dawn
> Shall come; – the shining hope of Europe free:
> The league of sober folk, the Workers' Earth,
> Bringing long peace to Cornland, Alp, and Sea.

I moved then into the final stanza with what I hoped would be perceived as a subdued intensity. Mrs. Houston had given me the phrase: *subdued intensity.* "It breaks his heart," I said, having made *eye contact* once again with the judge, "that kings must murder still . . ." And I concluded the poem with an intensity that I believed was precisely and appropriately subdued.

When it was my turn to meet with the judge, she and I alone in the same room in which the readings had taken place, I could scarcely contain my excitement. Yes, I had come to the festival, had decided to compete in the Oral Interpretation: Poetry category because I wanted a respite from my classes, from my routine, and, yes, I wanted to experience the sights and sounds of a town much larger than my own. But little by little, as I read and reread the poems, both at home in my bedroom and at school in front of my classmates, I became competitive – until the possibility of receiving any rating lower than superior became unthinkable. I refused to imagine that any of my peers might outdo me, that Donna Davis or Phyllis Harnden, for example, might receive a higher mark on their prose than I on my poetry, or, heaven forbid, that Farrel Paulk with his excerpt from a Shakespearean play whose title escapes me might be the only male to represent my high school at the state festival in Topeka. Nevertheless, I do hereby swear that when I threw my hat into the regional speech festival ring I did it purely on a lark, intending only to go along for the ride.

But things change, don't they? Now, sitting on a folding chair facing my judge, waiting for her to critique my presentation and to tell me the rating it had earned, I was nervous and suddenly profoundly apprehensive.

My judge smiled. She was indeed handsome, her face square-featured, her dark hair wavy and thick. She was tall and small breasted. She sat straight-backed and regal on her chair, her throne, her legs crossed, the clipboard in her lap. I could see that the pad was filled with notes, some of them written at odd angles.

You have a fine, rich voice, she said. Hers was pretty much alto.

I tried to smile. She talked some more about my voice, about resonance and what she called *timbre*, and I began to relax. She rarely consulted her notes, which meant that most of the time we made *eye contact*. She wore no lipstick, and there were several large freckles across her nose. She said that she found my voice convincing – that is, it seemed to her plausible as the voice of a man speaking as a citizen of early-twentieth-century Springfield, Illinois. Most boys in high school, she said, sound like boys in high school, regardless of what they might be reading. But my voice sounded like a man's voice, and that, she said, constituted a distinctive plus.

I nodded and tried to smile. Boy howdy.

And you handled the language in the poem with ease and facility, she said, and somehow I knew that no matter how long I might live I would never forget *facility*, never forget how she said it, how sweet it sounded, how it lay on that distance between us like something soft to touch or to walk on, and she mentioned some of the language that I had handled with facility, some of it the same difficult language that I had stumbled over when I first encountered the poem – "quaint great figure" and "dreadnaughts scouring" and "shawl-wrapped shoulders." She said, too, that I had paced the reading effectively, and that I had given each word, each phrase, its appropriate intensity, and . . .

My nodding was intended to indicate less agreement with than appreciation of what she was saying. Appreciation – and embarrassment, too, because I had not expected such a litany of strengths.

Nor did I expect the following question: At the end of the poem, Mr. Kloefkorn, why did you drop your voice?

I did not know how to respond because I was not aware that dropping my voice at the end of the poem made any difference, one way or the other.

She smiled at my silence, then repeated the question. I offered additional silence, then at last I said, I don't know. I always read it that way.

My judge smiled, but not widely. Then, still smiling, she said, The poem ends with a question, Mr. Kloefkorn, doesn't it? Can you remember how the poem ends?

I nodded. She was looking at me, making *eye contact*, her smile reduced but not altogether extinguished. She seemed to be waiting not only for me to remember, but also to recite. So I inhaled deeply and gave her the entire final stanza:

> It breaks his heart that kings must murder still,
> That all his hours of travail here for men
> Seem yet in vain. And who will bring white peace
> That he may sleep upon his hill again?

There, she said, you did it again. You dropped your voice. You should not drop your voice when you ask a question, Mr. Kloefkorn. Should you?

I thought about it – then thought a little bit more. No, I concluded, I probably should not have dropped my voice. But isn't it terribly difficult to elevate the voice at the end of a rather long sentence?

It *is* terribly difficult to elevate the voice at the end of a rather long sentence, Mr. Kloefkorn, agreed my judge. But the elevation indicates uncertainty, and surely the voice in Mr. Lindsay's poem is woefully uncertain. It wonders whether "white peace" will ever become a worldwide reality. Its lack of certainty underscores its frustration.

Then to illustrate her point she recited the poem's final sentence, her alto clear and strong and utterly professional. At the end of the sentence she elevated her voice so that the question hung in the air like something heavy unable to descend in spite of its heaviness.

You understand? she asked, and I nodded because I did in fact understand, though later, thinking about it, I did not at all understand how Molly Cloud Houston had overlooked such an obvious aspect of Vachel Lindsay's poem. I had overlooked it myself, perhaps because it was easier to speak the sentence without elevating the voice, or because I thought – and maybe Mrs. Houston likewise thought – that a lowering of the voice was sufficiently effective.

It pains me to lower your rating from a superior to an excellent, said my judge. But I must do it.

She smiled. I nodded.

She gave me a sheet of paper that in the bathroom I reduced to confetti. Later, walking the main street of Pratt, Kansas, I wondered if anyone else in the history of humankind had ever been treated so harshly by way of honesty. And into this dubious bargain Farrel Paulk had read the excerpt from his play so flawlessly that probably already he was looking forward to Topeka. The month was April. The afternoon was bright and windless and aromatic. Pausing to do some window-shopping at a store displaying model airplanes, Duckwalls maybe, I rethought my plight, and to satisfy my lust for both irony and consolation, like Lindsay I decided to end with a question: Do you suppose that anyone in the history of humankind has ever been treated so harshly by way of honesty?

The second poem that refuses to escape my memory is Edna St. Vincent Millay's "Dirge without Music." This was another of the half dozen I had practiced for the speech festival. The voice in this poem is that of the poet herself as she refuses to accept what in the opening line she calls "the shutting away of loving hearts in the hard ground." I had rehearsed this poem, as I had rehearsed the others, in my bedroom, alone, yet when later I read the poem in front of my classmates I did so with considerable trepidation – because the poem is filled with what Molly Cloud Houston will identify as *caesuras*, pauses within the lines, and I didn't know how long I should pause or whether the lengths of the pauses should vary. Then, too, there was the matter of seriousness, or solemnity or, heaven help me, *portentousness*. Quite clearly the tone of the poem, the poet's attitude toward death, is a sober one. But should the soberness be emphasized to the extent that it suggests anger? Bitterness? Hostility? In my bedroom, alone, I had tried a variety of approaches, softening my voice as I read.

> They have gone to feed the roses. Elegant and curled
> Is the blossom. Fragrant is the blossom. I know. But I do not approve.

Then – because my voice is sometimes baritone, but most of the time bass – I spoke the first two lines of the final stanza slowly, beginning with a moderate baritone that ended with my best basso profundo:

Down, down, down into the darkness of the grave
Gently they go, the beautiful, the tender, the kind ...

How emphatically should I speak these lines? "Gently" at the start of the second line indicates – well, gentleness. But the poet is dissatisfied. So where is the reasonable middle ground between gentleness and dissatisfaction?

When I first read the poem in class I was certain I had read it too rapidly – or too unevenly or perhaps too quietly or too dramatically or ... But line by line I managed to struggle through, though by the time I reached the final stanza I was unable to make *eye contact* with any of my classmates; they were looking at something off to my right and slightly behind me, and what had caught their attention was Molly Cloud Houston. She was crying. And, in spite of the tears, she was smiling.

I turned to look at her as soon as I had read the final line of the poem: "I know. But I do not approve. And I am not resigned."

I did not know how to react. I felt personally responsible for Mrs. Houston's condition, but I could not imagine what I had done to provoke it. Here was a beautifully blue-haired woman, my English teacher, sitting at her desk, weeping as she smiled, and here was an unwashed reader-of-poems standing like a misplaced lummox in front of his bewildered classmates wondering what in the name of all that is holy or ever hopes to be he had said or done to bring about such an embarrassment.

Locating a handkerchief, Mrs. Houston dried her eyes as she continued to smile, her round cherubic face dimpled like a baby's. Astonished, I watched her in silence, as did the other members of her class. Perhaps, with me, they felt somehow responsible, as if collectively we had schemed to torture and abuse our teacher because however kind and instructive she might have been she was, after all, our teacher. And now that we had pulled off our dastardly plan, whatever it was, we were wondering if, after all, we had accomplished anything. In any case, we watched with our tongues tied as Mrs. Houston composed herself.

5

The process of social change is epitomized in the fact that the first Packard car body delivered to the manufacturer had a whipstick on the dashboard.

—Helen Merrell Lynd, *Middletown*

The bluebird carries the sky on his back.

—Henry David Thoreau, *Journal*

O! for a horse with wings!

—William Shakespeare, *Coriolanus*

Edna Hatfield. Her face resembled Mrs. Houston's, and so too her demeanor. She smiled a lot, and widely, and her cheeks, like Molly Cloud's, dimpled when she smiled, the depth of the dimples depending upon the width of the smile. Her hair was not blue, but white – white as a new snowfall – and the flesh on her upper arms jiggled impressively when she worked a mound of bread dough, as she often did, she being the premier cook in my parents' cafe and probably the best maker of pies in all of Harper County. She was married to a man much older than she, a tall big-boned cowboy whose retirement many years ago had not diminished his love of horses. He no longer rode his beloved horses, of course, but sitting at the counter nursing a cup of hot, black coffee, or trying to roll a cigarette, he enjoyed talking about them. And I enjoyed listening. He was a kind man with a gruff voice, and he rarely turned to look me in the eye. Instead, he would talk to his coffee, or to the tissue he was attempting to fill with tobacco, telling it stories of his days as a rider and a roper, of his favorite mounts, including their names – Sadie and Hacker, Blue and Jody and Cheyenne.

I'd sit beside him on a high stool at the counter, eating a substantial wedge of Edna's banana cream pie. I'd nod occasionally, maybe saying a word or two to let him know I was listening and was interested, and he would continue until the coffee he'd sip between stories was gone, or until he gave up on rolling the cigarette, which eventually he always did because he couldn't control the tremor in his left hand. These would be slow times in the cafe, a weekday afternoon, say, and I'd have washed all of the dishes and cleared and cleaned the booths and the counter. Back in the kitchen Edna and my mother would be putting things in order for what Mother quite accurately called "the supper run."

I remember when I asked Mr. Hatfield, William, if he had heard of the upcoming race between John Barker's horse and Chet Black's new Packard.

No, he said, and his ears, which were inordinately large, quivered and slightly reddened as I gave him the details – how I knew that Black had a new Packard, this one a two-tone, tan over dark brown, and how I had heard in the pool hall that Barker had challenged him to a race, one hundred yards, the track to be the high school football field, Saturday morning at nine-thirty sharp, winner take all, or so I had heard, though I did not know what *all* meant – a wad of money, probably, and probably a small wad, because Barker, an ornery small-time farmer who did most of his planting and reaping in the pool hall, was not very well fixed. But who cared? The bragging rights would matter more than the money, and in any case the challenge had been accepted, and the men had shaken hands, and now the news, and its attendant speculations, were spreading like wildfire by word of mouth.

Mr. Hatfield pulled a sack of Bull Durham from a shirt pocket and began the long and deliberate ritual of trying to roll a cigarette. Many times I had watched him tap tobacco from the pouch into a furrow of white cigarette paper, but I cannot remember seeing him finish the process. He would work at it until the counter was well seeded with tobacco that because of the tremor missed its mark; then, nodding his head affirmatively, as if to say that failure was precisely what he had expected, maybe even intended, he would clear the counter with a sweep of his large freckled hand, pull the strings to close the sack, and return the Bull Durham to its pocket.

Mr. Hatfield turned his face partially toward me, his mouth half grimace, half grin. Well well, he said. That should be some race. He had a bass voice with some gravel in it.

I agreed. I told him I thought I'd bet a dollar or two on Barker's horse. I asked him if he thought that was a good idea.

A new Packard, he said, speaking now to the sack of Bull Durham he was attempting to open. A new Packard?

It's a two-tone, I said. Tan over dark brown. What do you think?

What Mr. Hatfield thought was that the man who invented the Bull Durham sack should be gelded. I nodded. There was a sprinkling of tobacco on the counter.

He thought also that the horse would win, or should, because, he said, if it's a Barker horse it's a damn good one.

He was holding the sack of Bull Durham in his right hand, aiming its open end down toward the tissue he was trying to control with his left hand. With his right index finger he tapped the sack lightly until it released tobacco in the general direction of the furrowed paper. But as the tobacco hit the tissue the hand tremored, and the tobacco, almost all of it, fell to the counter. Nodding, Mr. Hatfield crushed the cigarette paper and with one sweep of his hand cleared the counter.

He did not tell me outright that I should bet on Barker's horse, but he made it clear that he was in Barker's corner; if Barker didn't know a tinker's good goddamn about most things, Bill Hatfield said, he knew a truckload about horses.

I had finished my piece of banana cream pie and wanted more, but I didn't go get one. Mr. Hatfield was telling his cup of coffee, which by now must have been somewhere between tepid and frigid, of the many virtues of horses in general and of Barker's animals in particular, though he knew these horses, he admitted, more through hearsay than observation.

And Chet Black has a new Packard, he said.

Yes, I said. Two-tone, tan over dark brown.

Well well, Mr. Hatfield said. Barker's horse and Chet Black's new

Packard. He steadied the coffee cup in both hands and, as if making a toast, said, Well well, that should be some race.

This would not be their first race nor would it be their last, not as long as Mr. Black could afford to buy a new Packard whenever he wanted. And he could afford to do the buying as long as his business flourished, and at the moment it appeared that his business might flourish forever. He had invented simplified versions of a grain auger and a one-way plow, had borrowed money, they said, to erect two large brick buildings where the augers and the one-ways were assembled. No doubt the time was ripe for the manufacturing of such implements, because they sold like hotcakes. Mr. Black's employees – and for a while I was one of them – could not put them together fast enough. Chet Black was on his way to becoming the town's first millionaire.

His passion, in addition to drink and occasional gambling, was the new Packard. He would buy one, abuse it for several months, then trade it in for another. His favorite method of abusing the new car was to use it to chase coyotes. He would remove the trunk lid and fill the space with a high, wide box made mostly of two-by-fours and chicken wire; into the box he would place a large, lean, mustard-colored hound dog he had trained to chase down coyotes. I was never invited to go along, but accounts of these chases were plentiful. Mr. Black and one of his cronies would load the dog in the improvised kennel and head for country that was more or less open, taking with them some whiskey and an assortment of guns – Black's favorite, a high-powered hunting rifle, and a couple of shotguns. When they spotted a coyote they would release the dog and then, no matter where the dog and coyote headed, the men would follow – over a pasture replete with rocks and bunchgrass and prairie dog holes, through a field of stubble, down and up a ravine with maybe a creek bed at the bottom, careening and bouncing and cutting cats' asses, the new Packard humming like a Singer sewing machine until something, a rock or a log, poked a hole in the muffler and the hum became a roar, the Packard now more nearly a low-flying piper cub than a vehicle, the men inside, having opened the whiskey, laughing and bouncing as the Packard bounced, the guns on the back seat bouncing also, the whole cock-eyed scene in front of them jerking up and down and sideways, dust streaming in through the open windows to coat not only the men but also the Packard's new upholstery, until sooner or later the coyote was cornered or run down or escaped, and the men would praise the mustard-colored hound and return it to its kennel in the Packard's trunk and maybe have another pull at the bottle before returning to the nearest gravel road to resume the hunt.

And when the hunt was finished, and probably with it the bottle, Mr. Black would take his roaring, limping, dust-laden Packard to the Champlin station where Hubert Hadsall would restore it, which might take several days, and by the time the vehicle emerged clean as new and sounding again like a Singer sewing machine, the story of yet another coyote hunt would have made the rounds from filling station to pool hall to grocery store to barber shop to maybe well beyond the city limits.

But each time Mr. Black bought a new Packard, and before he had a chance to rip off the trunk lid and insert a kennel, he was invariably challenged by John Barker: My horse Rusty, Barker would say, against that new piece of junk you call an automobile. Winner take all.

Barker might say some other things, too, to sweeten the challenge. You have the horsepower, he might say, but I have the horse.

Or: Turn away the challenge, he might say, and it'll prove what most of us already suspect – that you have shit down your neck.

Mr. Black would smile and shake his head, then shake Barker's hand, meaning that he did not have shit down his neck and that now the only things left to be decided were the time and place, though everyone knew the place would be the high school football field.

Saturday morning. Nine o'clock. I arrived at the football field thirty minutes early. Already the home stands were half full, and there were others, mostly men with some occasional children, standing along the fence that separated the stands from the playing field. Saturday in my town was always an active day, grocery shoppers and men waiting their turns for shaves and haircuts and other men at the filling stations fussing over their vehicles, kicking tires and spitting and lifting hoods, and somewhere around midafternoon a drawing, the winner taking not quite all but nonetheless taking away a substantial sack of groceries, and at night a double feature at the Rialto and a convivial cluster of men in Butch Mischler's pool hall playing pitch and dominoes and pool and snooker while their wives concluded their shopping and stood in groups in front of the stores talking about whatever women talk about when they stand around talking, so the race between Barker's horse and Chet Black's new Packard only added frosting to a multilayered cake. And the April morning was bright and windless, and I had put two dollars on Barker's horse, an anonymous buddy opting to venture his two bucks on the new Packard.

And Jesus Mr. Black's Packard did indeed look unbeatable. It was so new its owner had not yet had time to despoil it – no scratches, no dents, no cracks or dings in the windshield. Black drove it onto the field as if chauffering a chariot, if you can imagine a chariot with a hundred or so horses under a long shiny hood and a wide body that sat low and in a crouch, like an immense, predatory cat about to pounce. Mr. Black assumed a regal stance behind the steering mechanism, his back ceremonially rigid, both hands firmly on the wheel. He eased his chariot up to the goal line, its front bumper precisely at the line, and sat waiting for his competition to take its place beside him. From where I stood near the fence to the west of the goal line I could hear the motor running only when Mr. Black revved it, which he did from time to time as Barker turned his horse in a pageantry of circles before taking him to the line.

You look at the Packard, at its astonishing newness, its whitewall tires with their treads in zigzags deep and wide, and you almost have misgivings about your two-dollar bet with your anonymous friend. And you look at Chester Black, too, at what appears to be a figure with undiminished confidence, and though you know that he is more smoke than fire, and that he is probably two-thirds drunk, you nonetheless entertain the possibility that you are about to draw the stick with the shorter end.

But then you watch Barker atop his rust-colored horse and your confidence begins to return. Barker is a coarse, barrel-chested man who rarely stands very close to the razor when he shaves. He laughs easily and often. His teeth would tell you, if they could speak, that their owner chews tobacco, a lot of it, and when he smiles you cannot help but notice that the teeth and Barker's horse are identically colored. You watch this man so obviously at home in the saddle atop his horse, Rusty, reins in his left hand as he maneuvers his mount in circles in the general direction of the starting line, and you want to locate your anonymous friend and tell him that, if he doesn't have shit down his neck, he'll cover the additional two dollars you'll be dangling close to his anonymous face.

But more than anything else it is the horse itself that restores your confidence. You don't know much about horses, but you know that what you are looking at is an animal not only beautiful, Barker obviously having curried it to a high bronze sheen, but also an animal impatient to be given both the rein and the spur. You watch it cavorting in the end zone and the following words come to mind: girth, heft, muscle, haunch, nostril, eye. And piss and vinegar, because Rusty passes the one and exudes the other as prancing he lifts his forelegs uncommonly high, as if his prerace antics were being considered by a panel of international judges.

You move to the bleachers at the center of the field, find your way through an assortment of race fans to the topmost plank from which spot you can see clearly both the starting gate and the finish line. You look here and there, down the fence to the south and up the fence to the north, hoping but not expecting to see Bill Hatfield. He would be impossible to miss; his height, for one thing, in spite of a stooped condition brought on by age, would give him away, and if that didn't do it his black wide-brimmed hat would. This well-worn hat was an extension of Mr. Hatfield's well-sculpted head, and you have never seen him without the hat, would probably not recognize him without it. As he leaned into his cup of hot black coffee in your parents' cafe, his hat covered him like an umbrella, and when occasionally he turned to look at you, you saw a face that existed, you supposed, in perpetual shadow.

You are not surprised that Bill Hatfield isn't here. He is old and stooped and his daily trek to the cafe provides him sufficient exercise and entertainment. But you will take notes, mental notes, and from these you will give Mr. Hatfield a boy's more or less honest report of the proceedings, focusing upon what Mr. Hatfield will most appreciate – the look, the behavior, the performance of the one thing in the world that excluding his wife Edna matters most – the horse.

Now the moment for the race to begin is very near. Some shouting. Some jeering. An undercurrent of shuffle and buzz. With all of the others you are waiting for the starter to point his .12-gauge at an innocent and cloudless sky and pull the trigger. Mr. Black behind the wheel of his new Packard seems more relaxed, his left arm resting where the window would be if it weren't rolled down. Mr. Barker with short deft movements of the reins continues to exercise his lusty horse, continues to restrain it from exploding like an earth-locked comet across first the arena and then Harper County before disappearing over the horizon. Yes. You are going to win your bet. And Mr. Hatfield's large ears are going to perk up and redden when you describe, in some detail, the horse's victory, the automobile's defeat. Boy howdy.

It is uncanny to be looking over the field where only a few months ago I began my final season of playing football as a Bulldog. Where Mr. Black's new Packard is sitting is where we scored to defeat the Kiowa Chieftains, where we scored again to squeeze out a win against the Harper Bearcats. The line at which the contenders will finish is the one we crossed too many times almost to count as we humiliated Medicine Lodge. The field is comprised of rough grasses and weeds and compacted dirt, the feel and the smell of them lingering, prompting an ache that remains intimate beyond both desire and understanding. At the center of the field, precisely on the fifty-yard line, I had stood on a platform at halftime, the Homecoming queen beside me, and I gave her first a bouquet of red roses, then a kiss, not realizing that I was sharing honors with the young woman who would become the slightly older woman I'd marry and live with through four unprecedented children and an assortment of lovely grandchildren . . .

We had a successful season, in spite of the Kingman Eagles,

whose fullback, Gish, refused to believe that he was anything less than a tank left over from World War II, and the Caldwell Bluejays, who kept intact their reputation as the dirtiest team in the Southern Kansas League by breaking our center's leg. But we did something that a Class B team had never done before: We went to Wichita and clipped the almighty wings of the Plainview Cardinals.

Yet the best news, from beginning to end, was that we had a coach we looked up to well beyond admiration. He had graduated from Oklahoma State University, having played varsity football for three years, and unlike any other reverend we had served under he could practice what he preached – kick, pass, run, catch, and so on. In his padless uniform with a ball cap covering his premature baldness he looked like someone you'd welcome taking a chewing-out from. He was patient and thorough and precise and, excluding those moments when he preferred outspokenness, quiet. He had a small, impish grin that revealed teeth as white as Barker's weren't. And he had a wry sense of humor that took almost half a season for most of us to appreciate. His name was Spoon, Bo Spoon.

That win against Plainview gave our season a luster that not even time with its eternal rag can quite rub off. But then, alas, we moved into a season of basketball, and the worm not only turned but gyrated. We lost fourteen consecutive games. Losing became a ritual, a dirge pretty much without music because four of the band members were on the squad; relief, such as it was, occurred only at halftime as we looked to Coach Spoon for solace and for some tidbit of advice that somehow might open the door that some immutable force had closed and secured with a lock that had no key.

At home games the scene was this: Halftime. The Bulldogs are trailing Anyone by an impressive margin. The dressing room is an

94

upstairs cubbyhole soon to smell thickly of sweatsocks and jock-straps, hot violent breathing and impending defeat. Half of the team sits on a low bench, the other half on the gray concrete floor. Dry white towels are passed from one individual to another. Coach Spoon stands in the center of the room. He is a gracious man with many talents. During the upcoming summer, for example, he will play shortstop for a semi-pro team in Arkansas City. Even in the locker room, walking now back and forth, he moves like a shortstop, like a lean, well-conditioned cat. He snaps his fingers as he moves, and this snapping is another talent because having snapped first the fingers on his left hand, followed quickly by the snapping of the fingers on the right hand, he swiftly brings the flat end of his right fist against the palm of his left hand and the result is a distinctive *pop!* that is echoed by another *pop!* that results when he hits the inside heel of one of his brown oxfords against the inside heel of the other. Like all God-given talents, this one is difficult to describe. It is performed, at least as Coach Spoon performed it, without apparent effort – with *facility* – and when the dressing room is silent, or becoming silent as breathing returns to normal, the poppings provide a rhythm that soon enough many of our heads are nodding to. *Pop* and *pop* and – *pop. Pop* and *pop* and – *pop.*

When Coach Spoon stops walking and drops his hands to his sides we know not only that he is going to say something but we know also what he is going to say. He has no panacea to cure our collective ache, no advice that might open the lock for which there is no key. His homily instead comes in the form of encouragement that serves as solace. We are doing all right, in spite of the score. We are hustling and must continue to hustle. We are running the two-one-two zone defense pretty well. We are doing a fine job of getting the ball into our center, Woods (who, though not much taller than our forwards, who are not much taller than our guards, has a lovely high-arcing hookshot). We are . . .

And always, shortly before the buzzer calls us back to action, he offers the following: And one of these nights, boys, if we keep our dobbers up and our hands in the faces of our opponents, we are going to jell.

And we did. Game number fifteen, against the most formidable team in the league, the Medicine Lodge Indians.

Because the school bus had a broken axle we drove the twenty-two miles to Medicine Lodge in three cars. I found myself sitting in the backseat of Coach Spoon's Chevrolet, a blue and white four-door, eight-cylinder Chevrolet whose upholstery recently, probably when Coach bought the car, had been sprayed with something that made it smell brand new. In front of me, at Coach Spoon's right, sat our star forward, Evan Bullard, and at my left sat the center with the lovely looping hook shot, Gladden Woods. We had heard rumors that to a small degree lifted our spirits: Two of the Medicine Lodge star players were ill with the flu. One was B. H. Born, the Indians' center, who as a senior was trying to become seven feet tall, and who, though he would never quite reach his goal, would nonetheless become a starter for the University of Kansas early in his junior year, and the other was Tim Reichard, a forward who was not far behind Mr. Born. We told each other that we hoped the rumors were false, that we wanted to upset Medicine Lodge while the Indians were at full strength, but even as we spoke, now knowing that neither Born nor Reichard would be playing, we could feel our spirits coming alive and crawling slowly upward.

Jot this down: It is easier to jell when the opponent's two star players are not playing.

Even so, we very nearly lost the game. Neither team had employed the fast break, and both had been carefully deliberate on offense. The Bulldogs trailed at halftime, 23–21, but after Coach Spoon had snapped his fingers and clicked his heels in a rhythm we admired and respected and had assured us that if we kept our dobbers up and our hands in the faces of our opponents one of these nights we were going to jell, we returned to the court this time with more confidence than apprehension.

And it came down to this: With only a few seconds left, and the score tied, Gladden Woods, playing high post, lofted a lovely high-arcing hook shot that in memory if not in fact arose in slow motion to the peak of its arc, the ball's seams clearly visible, then in motion equally slow the ball descended to a spot just beyond the front lip of the basket where it hung suspended for the duration of half a moment before in memory and in fact it dropped into the net, fluffing it beautifully, and before it struck the polished floor the buzzer had sounded and the game was over.

Disbelief is difficult to deal with, even when its cause is reason for celebration. But we had not celebrated for such a long time that perhaps we had forgotten how to go about it. Coach Spoon was grinning, and so too was Woods, who surely was the shyest and the most modest center in the history of high school round-ball. I suppose that the rest of us were grinning too, and as our memories of celebrations began slowly to restore themselves, to work their ways from the abysses of our brains' lizard levels to the upper reaches of our neocortexes, we began to slap each other on our backs and whoop and insinuate our fists into the atmosphere and speak to each other, and to the universe, in tongues derived from the heat of victory.

And I remember how comfortable, how serene I felt as sitting in Coach Spoon's Chevrolet, returning home, I rethought the final moments of our momentous upset. Medicine Lodge, leading the league, had suffered its first – and what would be its last – defeat of the season, and though its stars had been lying in oversized beds while the Bulldogs were humbling their teammates (final score, 48–46), their coach nonetheless had fielded five players, which in the minds of some, perhaps many, should have been enough – stars or no stars – to whip that sorry quintet from that sorry hamlet twenty-two miles to the east.

But a victory is a victory, isn't it? We asked each other this question many times (more often than not rhetorically) that night and thereafter, knowing each time the answer: You goddamn betcha.

Coach Spoon's reconditioned eight-cylinder Chevrolet purred like a spoiled-rotten housecat. I remember that. And I remember that we sat in the same places we had occupied on the trip to Medicine, Bullard up front with Coach Spoon, Woods beside me at my left. And I remember too that there wasn't much conversation; for one thing, Woods rarely started a conversation, or did much to keep one going, because he was so shy and so equally humble, and for another thing I believe each of us was lost in the sweet improbability of what had taken place.

We were halfway to Sharon, about halfway home, when Bullard at last broke our trances. Clearing his throat, which was second tenor, he turned to Coach Spoon and said, Coach, how does it feel to win your first basketball game?

Bullard had asked a question that probably had gone through all of our minds – because it must have been an incredibly long and infuriating stretch for him, too, for any young coach out of Oklahoma State University who was on the job for his first year.

Finally Coach Spoon turned his head slightly, giving me a good view of the small grin at the right corner of his mouth, and he said, almost whispering, It feels like a bluebird just flew out my asshole.

You know the race is actually going to start, and very soon, when Eldon Martin with a .12-gauge appears and takes his place on the goal line well off to the west side of the contestants. Martin is a short frisky wheat farmer whose theology keeps him out of the pool hall and excludes him from a variety of other entertainments. But he is a very civic-minded person, too, upbeat and friendly and eager to serve, and he takes great personal delight in being a part of almost any project that might be viewed as a boost to the community. And he does not object to hearing his name mentioned when the project is finished and successful and is being reviewed and rehashed by his fellow farmers and townsmen.

You watch as Barker reins his stallion to the starting line, Chet Black at his right stoic behind the wheel of the gleaming Packard, watch as Eldon Martin raises his weapon deliberately and like a guardsman preparing to squeeze off a salute aims it at the vast blue sky as if he had seen something alien in the blueness that needed to be picked off. The onlookers go silent, anticipating the starting shot. And when you hear it you join the others in a whoop as you strain not to miss so much as a moment of the swiftly moving scene before you.

Barker's bronze stallion explodes from the goal line, his hooves dislodging a shower of divots, clumps of good gridiron earth, several of which splat against the Packard's windshield – because the Packard is not yet moving, Mr. Black having given the multitude of horses under his vehicle's hood more gas than necessary, and the Packard's rear tires in spite of their deep wide treads spin ruts into the dirt until Black eases up on the accelerator and the treads suddenly bite and the Packard, that crouching cat, lurches forward and though you have begun to believe the horse will have an easy time of it you begin now to wonder, Barker's stallion crossing the fifty yard line but being gained on, behind him the grill of the

Packard grinning, you with wide eyes not blinking, not wanting to miss a moment, Barker leaning forward, looking like a well-fed jockey attempting to protect himself from an onrush of wind by hiding behind the horse's flowing mane, Black's left shoulder and a portion of his head the only parts of him visible, his Packard gaining on the stallion, or so it seems, the contestants now maybe in a dead heat, you can't tell for certain, and if you had an instant to spare you might remember the legend of Attila the Hun, how nothing green that had been passed over by his mighty horse's hooves ever grew again, and when Barker's horse stops on a dime in the end zone you know that probably he has won, Chet Black in his Packard losing, you believe, but not by much, not more than a whisker, his massive steel animal then not able to stop as suddenly as did the stallion, meaning that the vehicle with its brakes set careens across the end zone and beyond it until drag at last prevails over thrust and the beautiful Packard comes to a stop and for a few moments sits sideways, Mr. Black behind the wheel like a remarkably overgrown infant in its cradle, rocking.

Whoops and jeering, and a youngster launches a paper airplane into the stratosphere and another runs along the fence rat-a-tat-tatting it with a stick and someone who can whistle with his fingers in his mouth whistles and Jesus H. Christ, Virgil, wasn't that the goddamnedest race you ever saw?

6

Parting is all we know of heaven,
And all we need of hell.

—Emily Dickinson

The camera photographs the cameraman.
—John Ciardi, "On a Photo of Sgt. Ciardi a Year Later"

. . . but O alas! in life we are in death.
—Gary Gildner, *Letters from Vicksburg*

No, Virgil said. Because I wasn't there.

You wasn't there? asked Stocker. Where the hell were you?

Waiting for a shave and a haircut, said Virgil. And I'm still waiting.

I was in line too, waiting my turn. The race had been over less than an hour, long enough for the relentless reincarnations to begin.

It was a ball-buster, offered Leland Bonham.

Especially for Barker, Stocker said. You see how fast that horse of his stopped once it passed the finish line?

On a dime, said Leland. Stopped on a dime, and gave Barker a nickel in change.

Sorry I missed it, Virgil said. But I was somewhere waiting to get a shave and a haircut.

Urie took a break from his scissoring and looked at Virgil. He grinned, showing a random assortment of oddly spaced teeth. Urie was a short thin man with gray hair and long fingers that he kept steadied with occasional trips to the back room.

You're next, Virgil, he said, and he looked at me and winked. Right after Cloyd and Leland. Just keep your shirt on.

Virgil's shirt was blue. He owned and operated the hatchery. His voice was deep and sonorous. Well, he said, it's a damn good thing I have more time than money.

You better have plenty of money, too, said Stocker. The price of shaves and haircuts just went up — didn't it, Urie?

Urie nodded. He was cutting the hair of someone I didn't know, someone whose expression was a blend of interest and confusion.

A lot had happened since the race ended. I had gone to our cafe to help with the noon run, and I had hardly walked through the door to the kitchen when Mother told me of Bill Hatfield's death. Heart failure, she said. Around ten-thirty. Edna won't be in until probably next Wednesday. You'll need to help Patsy wait on the tables as well as try to keep the dishes clean. But first, go get yourself a haircut.

I said I would, but I didn't go right away. I just couldn't believe that William Hatfield was dead. So I sat for a while at the counter, at the same place I had been when I told him about the race, and what I wanted now was to tell him how the race had ended, how Barker's bronze horse had bested Mr. Black's new Packard. I wanted to see his reaction. I knew that he would be pleased. I tried to imagine his face with a smile on it, and I tried to think of what he might say or whether he might let the smile do all the talking. I was still sitting at the counter, looking off into space, when Mother returned carrying two cherry pies that she placed inside a glass display case on the counter at my right. When I looked at her she nodded me toward the door.

So I went to Urie's barber shop where I found a spot at the end of the long bench that sat against the north wall. The place smelled sweetly of Sweet Pea talcum and bay rum. The several men who were waiting for shaves and haircuts were running then rerunning the race; those who had not attended the race did not hesitate to correct the observations of those who had been there.

Leland said, Barker shouldn't have won. That damn horse of his . . .

But, interrupted Stocker, his damn horse crossed the finish line ahead of Chet's Packard. Don't that make Stocker's damn horse the winner?

Barker's damn horse is a stallion, Virgil said.

So what? asked Leland. It's still a horse, ain't it?

And it crossed the finish line ahead of Chet's Packard, repeated Stocker.

But my point is that it shouldn't have, insisted Leland. Not if Chet Black had the brains he was born with.

The stranger in the chair was losing more of his hair than maybe he had bargained for. But that was the way Urie gave haircuts. He was a very considerate barber. Having given you plenty of time to settle yourself in the ample chair, and having secured what looked to be a bedsheet around your neck, he would ask you how you'd like your hair cut, and you would tell him, maybe saying "trim" instead of "cut," and Urie would nod sympathetically and when you were finished with your instructions he would proceed to fashion your hair precisely as he thought it should be fashioned, the devil take your instructions. It is possible, as some believed, that Urie knew only one way to cut a head of hair, so of course that was the way he did it. They contended that Urie asked each customer not so much how he *expected* his hair to be cut as how he would *like* or *prefer* it to be cut, which gave the customer the satisfaction of voicing his preference while at the same time giving Urie the option of cutting the hair the only way he knew how.

I watched and listened as Urie finished with the stranger, powdered him with Sweet Pea and doused him with bay rum before slicking down what was left of his hair with a fine-toothed comb; then, having untied the bedsheet and shaken it free of its many snippets, Urie grinning stood to one side, bedsheet over his left arm, to receive payment.

Chet Black no longer had the brains he was born with or, if he yet had them, for some reason was failing to use them (never mind his phenomenal success as the inventor and manufacturer of a simplified grain auger and one-way plow), because according to Leland he couldn't resist the temptation to spin "those goddamn whitewalls," as Leland called the Packard's tires, instead of easing "that goddamn house on wheels," as Leland called the Packard, away from the starting line.

You don't go anywhere when you spin your wheels, Virgil said.

You're telling me, said Stocker.

I'd like to have the brains Chet Black was born with, said Virgil.

My point is that Barker's horse wouldn't have won if Chet hadn't wasted half a goddamn century spinning his wheels, Leland said.

Virgil was in the chair now. It was his turn, in spite of what Urie had told him.

Anyway, Stocker said, Barker's horse crossed the finish line first.

Yes, and eventually I would collect two dollars from my anonymous friend, and before then I would be given a haircut precisely as Urie chose – or maybe had been unalterably programmed – to cut it, followed by the powder and the bay rum and the slicking down and the passing of coins from my hand into Urie's; and returning to the cafe I would be told that Mrs. Hatfield wanted me to give her a call.

What she wanted both gratified and surprised me. She wanted to ask a favor, and when I said, Sure, she said, I want you to take some pictures of Will. I'll have him at home in his coffin on Monday afternoon. Would you do that for me?

I didn't hesitate. How could I? Sure, I said. I can be there at four or four-thirty.

On the phone Edna Hatfield's voice was an extension of Edna Hatfield in my parents' cafe – soft, steady, confident without the slightest trace of self-importance. Mr. Hatfield had not been dead more than a few hours, yet already Edna had everything, or so it appeared, under control. The funeral, she said, would be at the Methodist Church on Tuesday morning, and would I take maybe two or three additional pictures at the cemetery?

My reputation as an amateur photographer was not extensive, but Mrs. Hatfield, as the principal cook and pie-baker at the R & K Cafe, had seen some of my work, including a five-by-seven glossy of the pie-baker herself, smiling her unpretentious smile into the lens of my new Kodak Pony, so she knew that I was handy if not yet altogether professional. And I remember how easy it had been to take her picture. She was busy over a pot of something, steam rising from the pot, and her manner of posing was very simply this: When I had her framed just so in the viewfinder, I would say her name, say it as a question – Mrs. Hatfield? – and she would look up and smile as if my calling her name had been a pleasant surprise and she wanted to know what it was I had in mind to ask her.

My darkroom was a small renovated storage closet near the bathroom, and the bathroom was itself a small room inside a space that connected the front room to my parents' bedroom, beyond which was the place where my brother and I shared a bed and a narrow chest of four drawers. These rooms ran parallel to the spaces in the cafe; before renovation, which was minimal, they had been used mostly for storage, though the front room could be used as a dining area for special occasions when the cafe proper overflowed. But when this room became our front room, with a couch and an easy chair and a coffee table and a couple of floor lamps, it could no longer be used as a dining room. The door that opened into the cafe had been left in place, making it easy to go between the front room and the cafe.

This was not the house, alas, with a floor furnace; that structure had gone the way of all the other places we had attempted to make a home in. But for two or three winters we had enjoyed the floor furnace, its clicking on when the thermostat so dictated, its warm air filling the living and dining rooms and to a lesser extent finding its way to the adjoining bedrooms, my sister's and my parents', then to an even lesser degree to the kitchen and finally to the far bedroom where my brother and I slept under several quilts and a blanket, and slept like stones, not really concerned that the warm air from the floor furnace had pretty much spent itself before reaching us.

We moved from this house to a ranch that for a year served as a playground for me and my brother and sister and as a failed experiment for my parents. We returned then to occupy another house, our sixth within the city limits and, when push came to shove, and we bought the same cafe we had sold when we moved to the ranch, we exchanged the sixth place for the seventh, that series of slender rooms that stretched, as did the cafe adjoining it, from the sidewalk on the main street to within some thirty feet from the alley. By then our family had been reduced by one; my lovely sister, having graduated from high school, had moved to Wichita.

Things for my family had not gone entirely to hell, but they seemed to be heading in that general direction. One house after another we were losing ground, one good house yielding to one not so good, then that one traded for another that in spite of two or three attractive features seemed nonetheless only a step or two away from – who knows? The rooms adjoining the cafe were compact, and always there was the aroma of something delectable in the air – fried chicken or roast beef or one of the several soups Mrs. Hatfield and my mother loved to concoct, potato or vegetable or ham and bean. And the jukebox music that moved through the wall that separated the cafe from our living quarters – most of the time it was pleasant enough, "Don't Fence Me In" or "Abbadabba Honeymoon" or the Ames Brothers with "Rag Mop" or Teresa Brewer with her sweet voice intoning "Music, Music,

Music." The sounds would travel through the wall all the way to the far bedroom to awaken me and my brother to tell us it was time to start thinking about getting ready for school. I enjoyed the pinball machine too, having it always so near, and the handy proximity of the drugstore and the pool hall and Urie's barber shop. But our string of rooms just off the main street, in spite of their attractive features, were more an extension of the cafe than they were a home. There was no place to sit down as a family, not if the family wanted some peace and quiet, maybe some time to talk something over; the front room with its large plate-glass window seemed more public than private, even with the curtain closed, and during the day it was impossible while in any of the rooms to escape the hum and clatter from the cafe. The cafe opened at six each morning, Sunday included, to accommodate the small town's early risers and, during the week, workers from the railroad's section crews, and it was kept open until after eleven o'clock to service night owls and stragglers, and to set things in order for the next day's early opening.

But there was something else, and you could see it in my father's eyes and hear it in my mother's laughter. Anger and apprehension had returned to my father's grass-green eyes, and traces of disappointment and spite also, the same small ominous signs that I had detected when Father went down into the storm cellar to begin the digging of the passageway for the installation of the floor furnace. And Mother's throaty laugh had too much throat in it, something sandlike and gravelly, a sound that told you, but subtly, that she had been crying. She was an expert at deception, my mother was. She would do anything to keep her children from learning certain truths, and the truth, one of them, was that she and my father would not be living together much longer. It was a truth whose withholding was no doubt intended to keep her children uninformed and therefore happy. But too often the throatiness in her frequent laughter gave her away.

In any case, when I told her that I wanted to go into the photography business she shook her head resignedly and laughed and told me all right, as long as I used my own money – which I more or less did, having saved some from the harvesting I helped with the previous summer, then later riding a John Deere as my fullback buddy Ray and I plowed under the wheat stubble on his father's farm.

I cleaned out the small storage room near the bathroom, sealed the cracks around the door, and acquired, though not all at once, the necessary equipment: one camera, a Kodak Pony; one safelight; one print box; three trays; one drying board; an assortment of developers and fixers; and finally, as a Christmas present, an enlarger.

By mid-April I had become proficient enough to have earned a string of small reputations, not all of them laudable. I had a reputation, according to my mother, for cluttering the premises with photos, photos enough, she said, to choke a Chinaman. And I remember wondering, Why a Chinaman? And how would a Chinaman, or anyone else, for that matter, choke on a cluttering of photos, or be choked with them? I also had a reputation for smelling like a darkroom, like the developing fluids and the fixers – especially the fixers, with their distinctive and somewhat acrid aromas. My girlfriend, whose parents owned and operated the other cafe in town, Bake's Cafe, would occasionally sniff the air and wonder, aloud, whether I had been spending much time lately in the darkroom. She was a short girl, and pretty, and our love transcended all impediments, including my smelling like a darkroom, so of course her question, and my response, was nothing more than a small bump on life's long highway to happiness.

I arrived at Mrs. Hatfield's house promptly between four and four-thirty on Monday afternoon. With me I carried my Kodak Pony and its flash attachment, the Pony loaded with film, my pockets loaded with flash bulbs. After classes I had gone to the track to practice throwing the javelin, after which Coach Spoon dismissed me early, after which I showered and dressed before combing those few strands of hair Urie had missed. I was wearing tan washpants and a blue pullover shirt with a yellow collar.

Edna Hatfield lived in a small square one-story wood-frame house two blocks west of the post office, which was two blocks south of the R & K Cafe. The front door faced to the east. By the time I reached the door Mrs. Hatfield was there to greet me, to take my right elbow and lead me into the living room. Several of her neighbors were seated in the room, and there in the southeast corner, located diagonally from the south wall to the west, was a silver coffin containing Mr. Hatfield; he was lying on his back with his hands on his stomach, one hand atop the other, and he was dressed in a blue suit and white shirt and a burgundy tie. Mrs. Hatfield was wearing a yellow cotton dress with a white flower pinned to a wide lapel. Her white hair seemed whiter than ever. She did not appear to be at all upset; there was a pinkness in her cheeks that gave her the appearance of someone younger than I believe she was, and she commanded the situation with poise and dignity. She introduced me to the visitors, told them why I was there, then directed them to retire outside where folding chairs awaited them on the lawn just south of the house. Bill needs to be alone with Mr. Hatfield, she said, while he takes the pictures.

When everyone had cleared the room I removed a bulb from one of my pockets and secured it in the socket of the flash unit. Take your time, Mrs. Hatfield had said as she left the room. There is no hurry.

I approached the coffin. Sunlight through a south window brightened the form of Mr. Hatfield – the blue suit coat, the white shirt, the burgundy tie. And the hands and face were brightened also, brightened to an unnatural shade of yellow into brown. There were deep creases in William Hatfield's face, and the upper portion of his forehead, because now he was hatless, was a pasty white, and the hair on his white head so thin I swear you could have counted the strands.

I did not quite know where to begin – that is, I didn't know where to stand to give me the best angle – so before I took the initial picture I tested the subject in the viewfinder from a variety of angles and distances. The strangest thing was that when I moved from one distance to another, from one angle to another, Mr. Hatfield's pose seemed to change ever so slightly, maybe because in each instance the silver coffin played a different role, and I was left to decide how important that role should be.

I had taken several pictures when it occurred to me that I should try one from an elevated angle, so I climbed atop a chair, a wooden one with a high straight back, and what I saw in the viewfinder pleased me, whereupon I took several more shots, moving the chair from near the coffin to a considerable distance from it, flashbulbs popping like the Fourth of July. I had moved into my work so intensely, was so absorbed by what I saw or did not see in the viewfinder, that I was well on my way to completing the assignment before I realized that I was talking to Mr. Hatfield as if he were sitting at the counter in the R & K Cafe, his black wide-brimmed hat shadowing his face, his eyes looking into a cup of steaming coffee. I told him that Barker's horse had won the race, had led all the way, I said, had left the starting line like a bat out of hell, I said, and when it crossed the finish line, I said, it stopped on a dime and gave Mr. Barker a nickel in change, I said, and I said you should have seen that horse, how John Barker had curried it to a high reddish shine, and how Barker rode that horse as if he, Barker, were a paid jockey and not an overweight, barrel-chested farmer, and how Chet Black's Packard having crossed the finish line went sideways with its brakes applied and finally came to a stop, rocking until it stopped rocking, and how . . .

My chief concern was that in spite of all my preparations – the Kodak Pony properly loaded, the wire from the camera to the flash unit snugly connected, each bulb tightly in place before the taking of each picture – something unforeseen and unexplainable would happen and I'd be standing in the darkroom nursing a long roll of celluloid blanks. Good God Almighty, what if this should happen?

But it didn't. I stood in the darkroom with the safelight softly glowing, and against that amber light I held a long strip of negatives that with the black and whites reversed clearly revealed the silver coffin and Mr. Hatfield lying serenely inside it – and good God Almighty some of the shots from those elevated angles were, no doubt about it, remarkable.

To be working alone inside a darkroom the size of a matchbox is a singular and gratifying experience, if the celluloid you are working with reveals something more than blanks. There is an intimacy that derives not only from the close quarters, but also from the faith you have in those materials you are working with, materials that like almost everything else around you, from electricity to that battery in your portable radio, you do not understand. You remove the roll of film from the camera, attach clips to either end, then with vertical see-saw movements you run the film strip through a solution of developer you mixed earlier in one of three trays. For a few moments your faith wavers, and the wavering does not desist until images begin to emerge, until enough of them are visible to indicate that your faith has been rewarded. You smile, though no one is there to see it, and probably you say something – to yourself, to the camera lying near the enlarger, to the images that like magic, like voodoo, are becoming more and more recognizable. In such a circumstance it is difficult not to indulge a sliver of vanity, difficult not to give yourself credit for somehow having been responsible for every facet of your success. Boy howdy. There lies Mr. William Hatfield, eerie with the black and whites reversed, eerie in the soft glow of the amber safelight.

You wash the film in another tray, fix it in the third, then suspend it from a taut horizontal length of wire. When it dries you will start the very serious business of making prints.

The prints tell you, finally, whether you have succeeded, and if you have you select the dozen or so that are the sharpest and that show Mr. Hatfield to his best advantage. At least half of these are the shots you took as you stood on the high-backed wooden chair, and one of them in particular, a closeup, reveals Bill Hatfield so clearly and so naturally that you are tempted to tell him again about John Barker's horse's victory.

But the choicest moments occur when you do the enlarging, when having exposed a five-by-seven sheet of Kodak paper you immerse it in a tray of developer and await the consequences. Little by little the image declares itself, Mr. Hatfield in his coffin rising ever so surely from the bottom of an uncharted sea. These moments are a blend of large and equal amounts of satisfaction and gratefulness. And you watch the image, your fingertips in the developer feeling the image, as if with the feeling you can coax it into a richer existence, until you believe its contrasts are precisely right, at which point you remove the paper from the developer to rinse and then to fix it before placing it face down on the sheet of aluminum that will give the paper, when it has dried, a high-gloss finish.

You do all of this on Monday night because you cannot wait to find out whether you will have something of quality for Mrs. Hatfield later in the week. Tomorrow you will miss classes to attend Mr. Hatfield's funeral, and later, at the cemetery, you will take several additional pictures, all of them without the flash attachment because there will be a high April sun, and Mr. Hatfield's plot will be under that sun, maybe twenty feet from the nearest tree. One of the pictures will show Edna standing near the coffin, one hand on its silver top, the other hand holding a single red rose. She will have been looking at the rose, studying it, and when you say Mrs. Hatfield? she will look up and bingo the shutter will snap and you will have Edna's lovely and incredulous face on a negative that will become a print that you will show her when the time is right.

And the time is right on Wednesday morning. I am so certain that Mrs. Hatfield – though she buried her husband yesterday – will be back in the kitchen, dutifully at work, that I take the folder of pictures with me when I go into the cafe to eat a little breakfast before going to school. Yes, there she is, standing in the kitchen, leaning over a mass of bread dough, working it, punching it and patting it, readying it to be the pie crusts that she'll fill with cherries and apples and peaches, creams of coconut and banana and chocolate, and the tart tang of lemon.

I love the smells and the sounds of our cafe in the mornings, bacon and sausage popping on the grill in the kitchen, the small clatterings of porcelain cups and saucers and the small talk all up and down the counter and maybe in two or three of the booths, if business is good. The section crew, of course, would have eaten more than an hour ago, by now would be back on the tracks pissanting their lining bars and manhandling their shovels and sledgehammers and spike mauls while keeping an eye out for the green board that tells them that very shortly a train will be moving through. At the moment I sense more than know what they will be doing because not until next summer will I learn such words as *pissant* and *lining bar* and *spike maul* and *green board*. I will have heard them, or overheard them, in conversations carried on by the gandy dancers themselves, or by others talking about them, but not until you have worked with Mr. Wilson or his equivalent do you come to appreciate the full meaning of each term.

I walk into the kitchen. Mrs. Hatfield?

She looks up, her hands buried in the mass of bread dough. Yes?

I have the pictures, I say, and I open the folder. The pictures are not glossies. I decided that glossiness did not somehow seem appropriate, so I settled for a flat finish.

Edna Hatfield smiles. Can I see them?

One by one, and slowly, I show her the photos, and one by one she approves, not by saying anything beyond *O my* or *Mercy*, and by nodding. I had selected the ten sharpest images and had arranged them in what I believed to be a reasonable order – the long-distance shots followed by the closeups, all of these taken in the house – but I do not yet show her the closeup that reveals a large man at rest looking almost too natural not to be talked to. Then I hold up the photos I had taken at the cemetery and developed just the day before, and Mrs. Hatfield, nodding, wonders if I might take a picture of the headstone in a couple of weeks, or whenever it might be in place. Of course.

She has not removed her hands from the bread dough. She stands erect, studying each photo, nodding and saying *O my* and *Mercy*. When I show her the one of her standing near the coffin, one hand on its top and the other holding a single red rose, she inhales deeply but says nothing. But when I disclose the final picture, the closeup of William Hatfield looking so peacefully natural, so apparently asleep, she can not constrain herself. She begins to weep.

I close the folder and step back. Edna Hatfield is weeping, but she is smiling, too, and suddenly her face becomes the face of Molly Cloud Houston who almost exactly one year ago sat weeping at her desk as I read Edna St. Vincent Millay's "Dirge Without Music." *They have gone to feed the roses.* And now I realize that neither I nor my classmates had conspired to torture or abuse our teacher. Time and circumstance had done that work for us. Youth and a fortunate absence of loss had prevented us from understanding and appreciating our teacher's reaction to the poem.

> Down, down, down into the darkness of the grave
> Gently they go, the beautiful, the tender, the kind . . .

Yes, and down go the old men also, and the women and their children and their children's children, and though the blossom of the rose is elegant and curled, and fragrant, *I do not approve.*

Nor does Edna Hatfield, I believe, yet she is smiling, and damn it all to hell the trouble with owning a Kodak Pony camera is that you seldom have it when you most need it – because when Mrs. Hatfield looks down at the bread dough, maybe to see if it is still there, then looks up and at me as if seeing me for the very first time, tears at her eyes somehow complementary to her smiling, I want to snap the shutter and take the image into the darkroom where I can bring it to life to show her – next week maybe, or whenever the moment is right – that some things must not ever be left to die.

7

And how am I to face the odds
Of man's bedevilment and God's?
I, a stranger and afraid
In a world I never made.
                    —A. E. Housman, *Last Poems*

The horizon's edge, the flying sea-crow, the
    fragrance of salt marsh and shore mud,
These became part of that child who went forth
    every day, and who now goes, and will always
        go forth every day.
—Walt Whitman, "There Was a Child Went Forth"

I therefore enrolled in college as perhaps the greenest of all freshmen, but not as someone utterly uninformed. I was familiar with two legitimate poems, legitimate because they had been published and had been selected for the Oral Interpretation: Poetry category, and especially the two poems I had studied most – Vachel Lindsay's "Abraham Lincoln Walks at Midnight" and Edna St. Vincent Millay's "Dirge Without Music." I was equally familiar with one poem not altogether legitimate: *It feels like a bluebird just flew out my asshole.* I was aware that essential information is information that for you is essential at any given time, that if you do not understand the denotation of *green board* you might well find yourself being hustled into the middle of next Wednesday by the cowcatcher of an unforgiving freight.

My greenness, then, derived chiefly from an absence of academic knowledge and exploration. I had read none of the classics, except through occasional comic books. I had very nearly failed algebra. I feared biology. I had never explored a college campus. I had never . . .

It is not surprising, then, that when I went to a defunct gymnasium to meet with my advisor I was approximately one hundred and ninety pounds of trepidation. The gym was located in a large, ancient, red-brick building, and it was teeming with enrollees, and most of them, it seemed to me, knew precisely what they were doing. Tables abounded, tables and papers and books and professors of all descriptions sitting at the tables – and looking like professors – and lines leading up to them and there I was, a greenhorn in tan washpants and a new Hornet sweatshirt purchased at the bookstore no doubt as a means of bolstering my confidence, of satisfying my quest for identity, there I was looking for my advisor, Professor Loy Banks, and having wandered about the maze until my greenhorn head swam I saw his name on a card on a desk and there wasn't much of a line so I didn't have long to wait.

Show me a gentler man than Professor Loy Banks and I will show you a saint. He was inordinately handsome, and dapper – slim and square-faced, with a Hollywood shock of hair, though he was not Hollywood. And, too, he was soft spoken. And along the way some Molly Cloud Houston had taught him the value of *eye contact*. With his perfectly blue eyes he looked at me and, having posed several casual, ice-breaking questions, asked me what degree I intended to pursue.

Degree? What degree did I intend to pursue? I did not know one degree from another, had no idea therefore which one to pursue. But I did not want to reveal the depth of my ignorance, which probably in ways I was not aware of I had already shown. But I said, I believe without irony, What degrees do you have?

Professor Banks was holding a college catalog in his right hand. Without bothering to open it he listed the undergraduate degrees offered by the college. The one that sounded best to me was Bachelor of Arts. So I said, Bachelor of Arts.

Professor Banks seemed pleased. He was a member of the English department, he had told me, and I suppose that a Bachelor of Arts degree fit his preferences.

Then you will need ten credit hours of a foreign language, he said. Are you proficient in a foreign language?

Not really, I said.

Then I'll need to enroll you in one, Loy Banks said, because I strongly recommend that you meet this requirement during your freshman year, five credit hours each semester. Which language would you prefer to take?

I hesitated. Who was responsible for having dug this hole, anyway? And who was too deep into it now to crawl out?

At length I said, What languages do you have?

Probably my responding to Mr. Banks's questions with questions of my own was the consequence of my experience in the R & K Cafe. Would you care for a piece of pie? Yes, I believe I would. What brand (or flavor or type or denomination) would you like? Well, let me see. What brands (or flavors or types or denominations) do you have?

Professor Banks, without looking at the book, listed several denominations, after which – without hesitating this time, because I wanted to appear self-assured – I said, I'll take French. (I'll have a slice of the peach, please and thank you, with one scoop of vanilla ice cream.)

To this hour I have no idea why I chose French. The logical choice would have been German; three of my grandparents were German, and one of them, my maternal grandmother, had come to America when she was seventeen. She met and fell in love with my grandfather and that was that. She never returned to the old country, though she spoke often about it, about the farm on which she was raised and about the many relatives who yet lived on the farm or near it, near Karlshuld, not far from Munich. When I was a boy she tried to teach me some of her language, but the Second World War was raging and I did not want my buddies to think I was being sympathetic to the Krautheads. And maybe a thin filament of this fear, of this bias or attitude, was yet somehow connected to some part of my greenhorn brain, causing me to say, and without hesitation, I'll take French.

Professor Banks smiled and nodded and filled in a blank on a schedule that only a few minutes later he had finished. Fifteen credit hours, he said, which is, he said, a standard load, meaning that if I carried a standard load each semester for eight semesters I could graduate in four years. I see, I said, though I'm not at all certain that I did. Eight semesters? Four years? Isn't that roughly the equivalent of eternity? And what happens if I fail my French course, or, what is even more likely, my biology laboratory? To what extent might eternity be prolonged?

But thanks to Professor Banks my apprehensions were considerably allayed. He was calm and gentle and poised – and he seemed to have no reservations about my ability to pass my courses, all of them, including French and biology. Perhaps I had fooled him, after all.

He instructed me to take my schedule and present it to those individuals who were superintending the appropriate tables, beginning right here, he said, with English – whereupon he gave me a card that, he said, guaranteed me a space in Freshman Composition.

I had some difficulty locating the appropriate tables, but with my schedule in hand, and my conversation with Professor Banks behind me, I felt a distinct lowering of trepidation and a gradual rising of confidence. So jot this down: In the midst of apparent mayhem, it is sometimes wise to stand aside for a moment and, with your schedule in one hand and your guarantee of a space in Freshman Composition in the other, count your blessings.

1) You have a warm, cozy room in which to study and sleep, a room that you will share with two buddies, both of whom are somewhere in this defunct gymnasium sharing its mayhem with you;

2) In your right hand you are holding a schedule that represents the first significant rung on your ladder of higher education;

3) You have a girlfriend back home, the middle daughter of the man and woman who own the other cafe in town, daughter whom

one day you will marry and with whom you will raise four children, two girls and two boys who will give you eleven grandchildren, one of whom at an early age will declare that he dislikes patience because *it takes too long;*

4) You own a 1938 Chevrolet with a clutch barely two weeks old;

5) You are wearing a new off-white sweatshirt with a black and yellow hornet on its front because

6) You have money in the bank back home because . . .

Because Rex Anspaugh called you late one Sunday afternoon to tell you that he would be driving to Zenda in the morning to check out a job, and would I like to go with him?

Yes, I would. You damn betcha. And I don't really give a rat's fat ass what the job might be. I need the money. It's almost the middle of May, Rex, and I think I'll be going to college early in September, if not before.

Rex was already in college, in a small seminary-related institution in Springfield, Missouri. He was the son of the local Pentecostal preacher, so of course he was a hell-raiser, but not to any hellbound extent. He was too childlike and personable ever to be excluded from anybody's paradise. He was smart and, when necessary, devious.

Early Monday morning we were on our way to Zenda, twenty miles to the north, a town even smaller than my town, Attica. Rex, who drove his Ford too fast over the gravel roads, filled me in. He had come across a notice in the local weekly, the *Independent,* saying that workers would be needed to help build a grain elevator in Zenda, that the pay would be good, that interested parties should apply in person at a site located in the northwest section of town. He had called several others before he called me. Bullard. Woods. Carpenter. No takers. They all had other plans, or didn't want to spend the summer driving back and forth to Zenda. He thought of me, he said, because he had heard that I might be going to college, and he knew me well enough to know that I probably could use the money, which of course I could, as I had told him over the phone.

And who knows, Rex said. We might not get the job. You know anything about building grain elevators?

Not much, I said. Do you?

Nope.

If you have never been to Zenda, Kansas, you should not despair. At that time the village boasted a post office, a filling station, a cafe that occasionally might be open, and a pool hall. Rex drove us to the northwest section of town, a flat expanse shaded here and there by cottonwoods and Chinese elms. At the center of the expanse stood a small building in front of which a sign told us that we were looking at the future site of a co-op elevator that would be in place to service that part of Kingman County by July of 1951. Not far to the south of this building was a square hole, a crater the size of half a football field, its west side shaved down to roughly a forty-five-degree slope.

Rex parked the Ford near the sign and beside what I believe was an old Dodge, its green paint yielding to rust, whereupon we looked at each other, exchanged what-the-hell shrugs, got out of the car, and walked toward an open door, the only entrance to the building. A man wearing a hard hat was standing at a high table examining a large blueprint whose edges kept wanting to curl inward. When he looked up and saw us he removed his hands from the blueprint, permitting it to assume the shape of a scroll. The man had blue steelies for eyes and a face chiseled from leather.

We told him we wanted to apply for jobs as advertised in the *Attica Independent*. I'm Rex, Rex said, and this is Bill.

I'm Grady, the man said. We shook hands. You boys have any experience building elevators?

No, we said. Not much.

Good, Grady said. He went to a small cabinet and returned with two sheets of paper.

Fill out these forms, he said. You need pencils?

We nodded and Grady fetched us pencils.

You can start as soon as you fill out the forms, he said.

We had not expected this. In the first place, we doubted that we would be hired. We had not imagined that an absolute absence of experience, if not a prerequisite for the job, might be considered an asset. And certainly we had not expected to be put to work so soon. Neither of us, in fact, had bothered to pack a lunch.

It was obvious that Grady was the head man, though at the moment Rex and I appeared to be the only members of his crew. I could see no one in or near the crater, and the green Dodge, probably Grady's, and Rex's Ford, were the only vehicles in the area.

We filled out the forms and returned them to Grady.

Hard hats are optional, Grady said. You want hard hats?

We said that we didn't.

Okay then, Grady said. Here's what I want you to do.

He took us to the edge of the crater and pointed downward. Those wheelbarrows down there, he said, are for hauling dirt. The shovels are down there with the wheelbarrows. I want you boys to fill those wheelbarrows with dirt, then push the wheelbarrows up that incline there at the west side and deposit the dirt over there under that piss elum tree. You see that piss elum tree?

We said we did. It was not difficult to identify, it being the largest tree, piss elum or otherwise, on the vast expanse.

Okay then, Grady said. That's it. Noon break goes at twelve. We knock off at five.

Grady did not waste a lot of words, nor did he hang around to field questions. He was gone, back to the blueprint, I suppose, before we had a chance to respond.

We walked to the west side and followed the slope to the bottom of the crater, then made our way over loose, uneven mounds of earth to the wheelbarrows – two of them, each holding a shovel, as if Grady possessed not only brevity, but likewise foreknowledge.

My friend Rex Anspaugh was speechless, and so was I. We had been struck dumb by what just now I'll call *immensity*. Grain by grain the sand in our mental hourglasses was falling, and with it the passing of time, and with time's passing the realization that Grady wanted us, my God perhaps *expected* us, to tidy up the lower sides and the bottom of this crater, this gargantuan hole in the ground, to load its shaggy unevenness into the wheelbarrows to tote and shove them up the incline to dump them in the shade of that large piss elum.

You must understand that my friend Rex was almost never at a loss for words, maybe because he was the son of a Pentecostal preacher who was never at a loss for words. And, too, Rex was inveterately hopeful – not hopeful that one day he would find himself in heaven sitting at the right hand of the Almighty, because this for him was an indisputable certainty, but hopeful that things right here on this lovely earth would work out to his and perhaps a few others' mutual satisfaction and delight. But at the moment his faith seemed to be undergoing a severe test, evidence of which lay in his being, for once, at a loss for words.

For the longest time we stood immobilized in silence, two young men standing tongue-tied at the bottom of an incomprehensible abyss. Grady had not been altogether explicit in his instructions: Fill those wheelbarrows with dirt, then push the wheelbarrows up that incline there at the west side and deposit the dirt over there under that piss elum tree. The most elusive element of his instructions was the opening, Fill those wheelbarrows with dirt . . . Well, there was plenty of dirt here at the bottom of our incomprehensible abyss, dirt lying in irregular mounds everywhere, many of the heaps the result of earth having fallen away from three of the more or less vertical sides. But where do we start? Is there any plan, any pattern that we might be wise to follow? Or do we simply push our wheelbarrows to the nearest heap of dirt and begin the loading and the hauling and the dumping and . . .

And I thought of my father with the family shovel filling the calf bucket, then the lard container, with the dirt I'd tote up the earthen steps and out of the back porch and across the driveway to the plot of bunchgrass just east of the outhouse, where I would deposit the dirt, one bucket, one container, after another until a hill evolved, until the hill became the mountain my little brother ruled until his larger, older brother launched a flanking movement and kicked his little brother's little ass smack into the middle of next Wednesday, their father meanwhile on his knees in the cave, in that place for the storing of home-canned goods, chipping away at the dry compacted earth with the family shovel as he sang all the words he ever knew of "The Great Speckled Bird."

At last I said, maybe because of what I had been thinking, Well, Rex, there's a lot of dirt here, isn't there? But we don't have to move all of it out in one day, do we?

Rex grinned. He said, Shit no.

We selected wheelbarrows and pushed them to the nearest mound. From the rim of the crater we must have resembled two antlike aliens embarking on a mission that only aliens, or idiots, would dare embark on. But we embarked anyway, knowing that according to our foreman, Grady, we had at least one distinct advantage: We didn't know what in the name of anybody's hell we were doing.

For just a few minutes, brothers and sisters, let us consider not only the lilies of the field, how though they neither toil nor spin they become more splendidly arrayed than Solomon himself, even when he was at the peak of his glory, but let us consider also the olfactory and gustatory pleasures, and the attendant dangers, that can be derived from the inhaling and the eating of dirt.

At the time, several years before the outbreak of the Second World War, we lived in the house that I loved the most, a very small wood-frame structure that sat on a corner lot. And probably I loved the house not only for itself, for how its compactness enabled us to share our few good fortunes and our many miseries so intimately, but also because of its humility and generosity, its willingness to share its spot on that corner lot with space for an ample summer garden and outhouse, and space for a backyard that in turn yielded some of its space to a hand-dug cave my brother and I so frequently escaped to, its sagging roof a crisscross of pine boards and laths covered with tarpaper and feed sacks covered with some of the dirt we had removed to create the rectangular hole we so frequently sat in, its aroma in the nostrils ancient and damp and heavy, its taste that of a coin, of a buffalo nickel, perhaps, on the tongue.

But our cave, though it served us well during the summer, had to be abandoned when the snow began to fall and the north wind, down all the way from the Arctic, began to blow. During these days, home from school, my brother Johnny and I would search high and low for something to occupy our time. Father had attached a blackboard to the west wall of our combination living and dining room, and on it we drew pictures and played ticktacktoe and, if desperate, practiced our spelling and arithmetic. We browsed the Sears and Montgomery Ward catalogs, drooling over the pictures and descriptions of clothing and games beyond our means, and learning, at least subconsciously, the ins and outs of comparatives and superlatives: This cowboy shirt is *good*. This cowboy shirt is *better*. This cowboy shirt is *best*. We browsed until the catalogs, dog-eared and wrinkled, were relegated to the outhouse.

And on Sunday there were the comics, Smilin' Jack and the Katzenjammer Kids and Maggie and Jiggs, and the radio – with its static faithful as any servant – bringing us Terry and the Pirates and pilot Hop Harrigan ("cx-4 to control tower, cx-4 to control tower. This is Hop Harrigan, taking off . . . ") and the Lone Ranger and Jack Armstrong and my favorite, Tom Mix ("The Tom Mix Ralston Straight Shooters are on the air!"), whose horse's hoofbeats provided a syncopated accompaniment to the cowpoke's song:

Shredded Ralston for your breakfast
starts the day off shining bright.
Gives you lots of cowboy energy,
with a flavor that's just right.
It's delicious and nutritious,
bite-size and ready to eat.
Take a tip from Tom, go and tell your mom,
Shredded Ralston can't be beat!

These radio shows – aired each late afternoon, Monday through Friday – were a wonderful source of entertainment. And once in a great while there would be an event so momentous that my father would join us at the Philco – as for example the evening Joe Louis came face-to-face with an upstart named Billy Conn. It is the only time that I can remember my father cursing the static, though I have faith that he had done it before. We sat in a semicircle facing the radio, looking at the dial as if it were the ring in which the Brown Bomber and Billy Conn were about to touch gloves for the opening round. My father believed that Joe Louis was indestructible, and so intense was his conviction that all three of his children believed it too – and his wife, our mother Katie Marie, also seemed to share the conviction: She did not sit down, did not join our semicircle, but she paced the linoleum behind us, listening intently and wiping her hands again and again on her apron.

It is possible that our faith in Joe Louis was inspired by fear as well as admiration, because none of us, I believe, could imagine what Father might say, or do, should the Brown Bomber lose, and none of us, I am certain, wanted to be in the same county with Father should this happen.

And for twelve nail-biting rounds it appeared that this might indeed happen. The announcer's voice, laced with static, tallied the points round by round and told us who was leading. And at the end of the twelfth round Billy Conn, the upstart, was leading, was far enough ahead on points that, should he win only one of the three remaining rounds, he would be crowned the new heavyweight champion of the world. And certainly that was more than a mere possibility, because Conn was a dancer, not a knockout puncher. If he could continue to bob and weave, duck and feint and backpedal for three more rounds, the golden belt would be his. And Conn seemed to be getting his second wind, the announcer said, then repeated what he had said at least a dozen times – that Conn looked like a modern-day Gentleman Jim Corbett.

Father's anger increased as each round ended and the announcer tallied the points, but it was not a demonstrative anger;

instead, it was a displeasure characterized more by intensity than by any outward, blatant display. Father studied the radio between rounds almost as deliberately as he stared at it while the fight was being announced, his teeth clenched, his lips slightly open, his curses uttered in hisses and whispers too profoundly intense not to have been God-given.

And sure enough my father's intensity paid off. For some reason, probably because he honestly believed that he had sapped the strength of the Brown Bomber, Billy Conn decided – or perhaps his handlers decided for him – that he should abandon his jab-and-run approach and instead stand toe-to-toe with Louis. This fatal miscalculation soon left Conn flat on the canvas, and before he could find his legs the referee had counted him out and my father, true to form, showed his joyful amazement with only a slight smile and a clap or two of his hands. Son of a bitch!

But a major event like the Louis-Conn bout did not happen very often and, with so little to keep us occupied during those long winter evenings, it was probably inevitable that I would do something so foolish as to smash our living room window. At any rate, I did just that. It happened one evening at the height of a howling snowstorm as I was practicing a game called "slipper kick," the object of which was to kick one's slipper, or shoe, as far as possible. It's a simple game. You loosen the shoestring and then, with your foot only partially in the shoe, and the shoe directly beneath you against the floor, you balance yourself on one leg and kick the shoe as far as your strength and timing allow. It is perhaps not a skill that one should attempt to refine in one's combination living and dining room, especially on a winter evening when snow is falling and arctic winds are howling. And, too, when you practice the slipper kick inside a house, you can feel confident that the shoe cannot travel beyond the quilt that you have hung on the wall to cushion the blow – unless you manage to miss the quilt entirely and send your shoe through a window. To this day I do not understand how the shoe missed the quilt. But it did. And the arctic wind, looking I suppose to warm itself, entered the room uninvited – and continued to rush inward until Mother took down the same quilt the shoe had missed and used it to cover the space where the glass, now a glittering mass of shards on the floor, had been.

Go find some tacks and some tape! Mother shouted. She stood holding the quilt against the wind, her arms extended almost to the top of the window. Our stove, a coal-burner less efficient than the one we would later replace with a floor furnace, was already losing its battle with the incoming wind.

In a kitchen drawer I found both tacks and tape. Then, with the help of her three children, Mother soon had more or less secured the edges of the quilt to the wall, though she could not prevent it from flapping and billowing against the wind. And the amazing thing is that when Father came home from work and was told what had happened, and saw how tacks and tape had been used to hold down the quilt, he laughed until finally he had to reach into a rear pocket for a rag that in another life might have been a handkerchief. And that winter he did not replace the glass. Instead, he found two cardboard boxes and with them devised a double-layered covering that became another surface – the other was the blackboard on the west wall – for his children to draw and figure and scribble on, and to squabble over.

Once in a while, maybe shortly before Thanksgiving and then again before Christmas, someone would think of the box of pictures that Mother thought she kept out of our reach in a cardboard box on a high shelf in her closet. The pictures were black-and-whites – and a few sepias – of family members stretching back to my maternal grandmother when at seventeen she arrived in this country from near Karlshuld, Germany. Many of the figures in the photos were stiff and formal, we thought, dressed as they were in clothes that looked both odd and uncomfortable. A few were not so deliberately posed and thus more lifelike – a man sitting on the metal seat of a cultivator holding reins that led to a team of wide-haunched horses, or a woman holding a bucket of grain she was about to scatter to a few chickens milling about in the background. Mother would sort through the pictures, identifying some of the people and maybe saying something about where they came from or how we were related to them or what happened to them or what they were doing when the photograph was snapped, if we couldn't figure it out for ourselves. Eventually, of course, she would come across the picture that we most wanted to see, the one we called "Sumner's rear end."

It was a five-by-seven black-and-white photo with scalloped edges frayed from handling. It revealed Mother and Father posing out-of-doors, Mother sitting demurely on a chair obviously taken from the house, Father standing at her left with his hands in the pockets of a new pair of blue overalls, their legs highly cuffed. Mother, dressed almost all in white, was holding my sister, who looked more like a doll than an actual sister, and who was also dressed in white. And how old might the doll who was my sister have been? Two months, maybe, which means that the picture was taken sometime in October, Bernadine having entered the world, which was Kansas, in late August. It would be two years before my own birth and four years before my brother's.

It was obvious, even to us youngsters, that the photo had been carefully staged: Mother sitting in the chair holding my sister, Father standing close beside, and just behind them what must have been my parents' proudest possession – a shiny black coupe, a

Ford probably, clean as a whistle. Behind the vehicle were a bush and a small tree, both with only a few leaves hanging on, and beyond them a field of stubble stretching to meet the horizon, a seemingly limitless expanse entirely worthy of the Sunflower State. Probably a family gathering had prompted the photo, and surely the one who arranged it did not suspect that a dog – Mother had named him "Sumner" for the county he came from – would stand in the lower right-hand corner with only his rear captured by the camera. And just as surely the choreographer did not foresee the white kitten standing in the lower left-hand corner facing the camera, its tiny eyes wide open.

The photo puzzled me. I was puzzled because it offered visible proof that my sister was alive while I was not, that she was being held in the arms of my mother while I was nowhere being held by no one. I tried to imagine being nowhere, but I couldn't do it. Always there would be a place, and always someone would be there to further spoil my attempt to envision nothingness.

And the photo tickled me, and tickled my little brother, too, because it so clearly revealed Sumner's rear end. Mother had been the one to name the photo "Sumner's rear end," which meant that Johnny and I – and later our sister, who for some time failed to acknowledge the humor implicit in a sharply focused image of a dog's rear end, maybe because she too was in the picture – could speak the title of the photo with impunity. *Sumner's rear end. Sumner's rear end.* We would say it, and chuckle, and repeat it, and chuckle again – until Mother took the picture from whoever was holding it and told us to hush, and she meant it, and returned the photo to the box.

It gives you a warm feeling to be in a warm room on a cold night looking at old pictures, the flames in the coal-burner making its isinglass windows red as the devil's eyes. And the best part is the laughter, how maybe it starts as your little brother, holding "Sumner's rear end," begins to giggle, then giggle some more, until you cannot hold back and you giggle also, you saying "Sumner's rear end" just after your brother says it, and sometimes even your mother joins you, then your sister, and all of you are laughing at whatever it is that tickles you, and you think that if your father were here instead of outside working overtime for the county, operating a snowplow, probably, he'd be laughing right along with you.

But viewing Sumner's rear end, and reading the comics and studying the catalogs and listening to the radio and practicing the slipper kick were mostly winter entertainments that, though often fun, were very confining and certainly could not compare with all the carefree summer activities. Then, I had the run of the vast out-of-doors, those spaces on our modest acreage that so warmly and benevolently defined it--the backyard with its garden and hand-dug cave, and that space occupied by an outhouse behind which a pile of tossed-off lumber claimed its small but aromatic space, where mice and now and then a rabbit found room enough to establish their own modest homes.

And a space at the northeast corner of our property for a ramshackle barn, and between the barn and the outhouse another space – the cow lot.

And in those days our Jersey roamed this lot with a justifiable sense of ownership, it being the only cow on the premises. The cow supplied us with plenty of milk, enough for Mother and Father and their two sons, and enough for the sons' maternal grandmother and for their sister, who was living temporarily with the grandmother. The cow lot was encircled by a high fence nailed to creosoted railroad ties that served as posts. Inside the lot, not far from the east side, say twenty feet, stood an old cottonwood tree, and from one of its higher branches hung a frayed hemp rope, its lower end attached to a gunnysack we had stuffed mostly with fabrics from the ragbag, adding some dirt from the cow lot as ballast.

Because the rope had been tied to a high limb the gunnysack when in motion would describe a high wide arc, my brother and I taking turns climbing the fence to stand atop a convenient post to send the sack on a riderless arc and watch it return, then to jump at the right moment to land astraddle the sack and holding the rope with both hands to ride the swing down and up and away and down and up again, eyes sometimes closed, sometimes open, until our swing arc by shorter arc gave way to some mystical law of physics, and dizzy with the aftermath of flight we would sit on the stuffed gunnysack turning slowly, so slowly turning.

Until it came to pass that one late afternoon in July, after a rain that had lasted all night and most of the morning, my little brother suggested that we "go swinging," as he called it, and because neither parent was at home, and the sun now was shining, and we had nothing better to do, we found our galoshes, snapped them securely, and headed for the cow lot.

In addition to the Jersey cow we owned two hogs, one of them a pig, really, and the other a full-grown hog about to become bacon. These three – cow, pig, hog – had left the barn when the rain subsided to wander and root the premises, and their cloven hooves had kneaded the lot into a deep and impressive ooze. The soil was dark and thick, and into this fertile density the rain and the hooves of the animals had mixed an assortment of manures, some of them fresher than others, and this is the compelling mixture that Johnny and I slopped across on our way to the swing. And I must give credit where it is due: It was Johnny who suggested that we attempt what he called a "double dip," meaning that we would climb the fence together, one on either side of the post, and I would first stand atop the post and set the swing into motion and jump at and onto it when it returned, whereupon my brother, moving quickly, would scamper atop the post and when the swing and I returned he would jump at and onto my lap, such as it was, and with me would hold the rope as we swung down and up and away and down and up again, eyes sometimes closed, sometimes open, until . . .

O brothers and sisters, hear me! This is a maneuver that requires consummate defiance and timing. I must catch the approaching sack at the most propitious moment, of course, and of course my brother must do the same. But I must also somehow manage to be facing my brother when his most propitious moment arrives so that he might land on my legs; otherwise, his alternatives, neither of them very satisfactory, are these: 1) wait until I return again, and owing to the swing's describing a shorter arc be prepared to make a longer jump, or 2) jump anyway, intending to land not on my legs but astraddle the rope above the knot that secures the rope to the gunnysack.

It was all very complicated, certainly, very delicate, and no doubt these factors were partly responsible for my little brother's suggestion that we try a "double dip" – those two factors, and a significant third: the beautifully threatening – because sloppy – condition of the cow lot.

So with our overshoes snapped firmly in place we entered the lot and slopped our way to where the gunnysack hung like the head of a long lean unidentified snake in the shade of the cottonwood. We moved slowly because with each step the ooze threatened not to let go of our boots. Johnny, always fearless, led the way. The sky was mostly clear now, only a few billowy clouds off to the far east. And though the sun was not directly overhead it continued to do its work; steam was rising from the cow lot's muck as thick almost as fog.

Johnny seized the gunnysack with its long lean rope attached and carried it to the fence where he held it until having scaled the fence I balanced myself, squatting, atop the creosoted post, at which time my brother handed me the swing. Carefully, I arose to a full standing position. Below me Johnny was ascending the fence, preparing to mount the post the moment I jumped for the sack. And the operation, behold, came off damn near perfectly, my sending the swing on its riderless arc, the swing returning, my jumping to meet it, to straddle it and sail down and up and back down and back up toward where my brother stood; and, as planned, I approached him facing him and, his timing precise, he jumped and landed smack on my legs, and the gunnysack groaned and holding our legs out straight to avoid dragging them in the ooze at the arc's lowest point we flew like brotherly birds up and up in the general direction of a sky-blue heaven – which we did not reach, because O brothers and sisters, *damn near perfectly* means what it says, *damn near*, meaning that the knot that secured the rope to the gunnysack came loose and for the smallest fraction of a moment my brother and I sat, ropeless, suspended in the humid July air like cartoon coyotes until at a high sharp angle we fell like the essence of heaviness into the muck below.

Somehow we managed to land facedown in the slime and slid facedown on our bellies before rolling over to slide on our backs; finally having stopped we lay there in silence until the enormity of our baptism struck us, immersion so total we knew that its consequences might be total also; but before we could shower ourselves and our garments with the garden hose, hoping to avoid those consequences, we rubbed the mud and manure from our faces with the mud and manure on our hands, and when I opened my eyes I saw first the blueness of the sky, then my little brother standing over me, laughing, telling me that since he has had one swim

140

in our cow lot he might as well have another, so he bellyflopped back into the ooze; and the third thing I saw was our Jersey cow standing beyond where my brother was swimming, and she was looking at me looking at her, and what I should have thought, but didn't, was that she had seen what must have been for her an epiphany, a revelation not born from a yellow lunch bucket falling from the sky, as had happened to Mabel Cleveland's Holstein, but derived from having watched two young higher animals cavorting like the pig and hog she shared the barn with. And if the Jersey and Holstein could get together and compare notes, what conclusions or speculations, theological or otherwise, do you suppose they might come up with?

And with a cold rope of water from the garden hose we washed each other, and having donned dry overalls we hung our wet clothes on the line to dry, our wet boots with them, and when we told our mother what we had done she frowned before she smiled and shook her head, and that night and for countless nights thereafter the aroma of our adventure filled our nostrils, acrid and sweet, and the taste of mud and manure lingered, as such transgressions do, on our unsplit tongues. Amen.

8

I say therefore to the unmarried and widows, it is good for them if they abide even as I. But if they cannot contain, let them marry; for it is better to marry than to burn.

—Paul's first letter to the Corinthians, 7:8–9

According to Thomas Carlyle, *The healthy know not of their health, but only the sick.*

Rex and I were young and healthy and eager to please, but sickness in the form of aching backs soon told us that if we didn't slow down we would not last to see the end of our first day. I had implied as much before we began, had asked my buddy a semi-rhetorical question – We don't have to move all of this dirt out in one day, do we? – and Rex's answer, Shit no, should have confirmed the obvious: We must pace ourselves if we expect to live to work another day.

But we did not take to heart what should have been confirmed. We were young and strong and eager to please, weren't we, and we had a job to do, and in spite of the uneasy fact that we did not know exactly how to build a grain elevator we wanted to prove with our young muscles that we could do it, and that in the process we were more durable than dirt. So with our shovels we plowed into those mounds as if killing snakes, loading the wheelbarrows to overflowing, then like youthful sots we pushed them, wobbling crazily across the mounded floor of the crater to the slope at the west side, where like poor Sisyphus shoving his boulder up an eternal hill we urged our wheelbarrows up the incline to deliver our loads under the piss elum.

After a few trips Rex said, This isn't as much fun as I thought it might be.

I agreed.

We had started our loading by working in unison, watching each other in an effort to maintain a mutual rhythm, filling our barrows at more or less the same pace, then pushing our loads in a two-man file all the way to the designated tree. But by mid-morning our camaraderie had disintegrated, beginning when Rex said to the half load of dirt in his wheelbarrow, Shuck it, *shuck* being one of his favorite expletives, a home-grown euphemism that he no doubt believed would not unduly offend his and his church's version of God Almighty and, gripping the handles of his barrow he took off, leaving me alone with my own half load of dirt.

His decision to deliver only half a load of dirt to the piss elum each trip was prompted, I now believe, by either a flash of intellectual insight or a message delivered to him personally from the Holy Spirit. Rex was bright, charmingly bright, fully capable of figuring out that half a load of dirt would be only half as heavy, and thus easier on the aching back, and it did not seem to bother him that Grady might be watching and might not approve. Or his moment of insight might have been provoked by the Holy Spirit, because Rex as a Pentecostal was in perpetual contact with this Spirit, and because the Spirit was Holy, Rex moved when the Spirit so dictated, and more often than not the Spirit's instructions were explicit: Go ye therefore at a leisurely pace with only half a load of dirt and deliver it under the piss elum. Or words to that effect.

In any case, Rex at a leisurely pace delivered his half load across the bottom of the crater and up the incline where I watched him disappear over the horizon at the west end. And it occurred to me that if my buddy could get away with delivering half a load, then surely I could also. So shuck it, I did.

So we went our separate ways, each marching to the beat of his own drummer, until it was time to knock off for lunch. We piled into Rex's Ford and drove along the main street of Zenda until we spotted the one local cafe, which – perhaps to avoid the noon rush – was closed. But at the north end of the main drag we found a filling station willing to face that awful rush. We bought some

146

candy bars and some Tom's Toasted Peanuts and a couple of Cokes, after which we located what once might have been the village park – some dilapidated swings and a broken teeter-totter and a large rectangular hole that must have been the swimming pool. Three sprawling maple trees, however, had survived, and under the trees was a table made of two-by-sixes with two-by-six benches attached, and we sat on these benches and ate our candy bars, Power Houses and Milky Ways, and drank our Cokes and ate our peanuts and talked at length about the building of a grain elevator. And because Rex was involved with a young woman named Corrinne he talked a lot about Corrinne, mostly about whether in fact he might be in love with her; he knew for certain that Corrinne loved him, she called him on the phone incessantly to declare her love, and She's smart and beautiful, Bill, he said, and I knew that already. But I'm just not sure, he said, that I love her enough to ask her to marry me, not that I'm afraid of marriage, he said, but I don't want to go into marriage until I am absolutely certain that I absolutely love Corrinne, that she is absolutely the right woman for me, he said, and so on and so forth, and I knew without his saying it directly what it was he wanted – some sign or signal from his God Almighty that he was in fact in love with Corrinne and thus should declare that love and ask her to marry him.

When my Coke was half empty I poured my remaining peanuts into the bottle and using my thumb as a stopper I shook the bottle two or three times; then, removing my thumb, I raised the bottle quickly to my mouth and enjoyed an onrush of peanuts and fizz. I had been told that such a mixture was a poor boy's equivalent of bourbon and water, say, or gin and tonic. I did not quite believe this, of course, but I did not entirely disbelieve it, either, so each time I found myself with a Coke in one hand and peanuts in the other I gave the concoction a try.

It was good to be sitting at a table in shade provided by a triad of maples drinking Coke and eating peanuts and listening to Rex talk explicitly about his problems with Corrinne and implicitly about his needing God's assurance that he, Rex, did or did not in fact love her. Probably the moment was heightened because I too was involved with a girl, but the waters of our involvement were not muddied by divine uncertainty. They were not immaculate waters, by any means, not waters altogether free of the occasional mosses of doubt, but there was a deep-down clarity in them that provided me a certain measure of smugness as I listened to Rex examine his heart's dilemma.

We were careful not to overstay the noon hour. This was our first day on the job, and we had noted Grady's no-nonsense personality. So we were back with our shovels and wheelbarrows at precisely one o'clock.

We were wearing ball caps now, having decided when we returned from eating our candy bars and peanuts that the mid-May sun, though not yet scorching, was nonetheless intense enough to burn our foreheads; so we took the caps from the back seat, where we had left them when we got out of the Ford to enter the shed to talk with Grady about hiring on. Rex did not much like to wear his cap because it covered his shock of thick black wavy hair, and he was proud of that shock, and should have been; surely it must have been one of several reasons why Corrinne so loved him. And though Rex must have been aware of what the preacher says in Ecclesiastes – *vanity, vanity, all is vanity* – he had considerable difficulty wearing anything that might muss the hair that surely others enjoyed seeing. But the mid-May sun was hot, and the likelihood of sunburned faces did not appeal to either of us, so we returned to our wheelbarrows wearing our long-billed ball caps.

And soon we had returned to our routines, Sisyphus and his

unlikely twin shoveling dirt into their barrows until the muscles in their backs declared *Enough*, but still pushing the loads up the incline and dumping them under the piss elum. One leg over the other the dog walks to Dover.

At five o'clock Grady's voice was the buzzer that told us it was time to call it a day and, taking him utterly at his word I tossed my shovel into my wheelbarrow, which was almost half filled with Zenda, Kansas, earth, then walked with my buddy across the bottom of the crater and up the incline, this time blessedly free of a wheelbarrow. And I thought of how in some ways this day had been like those a few years ago when my brother and I carried dirt bucket by bucket up the earthen steps of our cave to dump it on a patch of bunchgrass just east of the outhouse. Then, we strained our backs moving small amounts of earth from one place to another; now, Rex and I had done pretty much the same, though on a somewhat larger scale. Nothing, then or now, to exercise the mind or challenge the imagination. Eventually, there would be a paycheck, if the back held up, and certainly that was something to anticipate. Then another week of shoveling and hauling and dumping, shoveling and hauling and dumping and doing then whatever Grady, or maybe someone else, told us to do. And suddenly it occurred to me that enrolling in college come September would be more than a good idea; it would be an outright necessity.

We moved directly to Rex's loyal Ford and entered it and took off our caps and tossed them onto the back seat and Rex started the car and backed it away from the sign that said that on these premises a co-op elevator would be in place by July of 1951 and we left the site with a spinning of tires that Chet Black himself might have been proud of had he been there to see it, which of course he wasn't, he no doubt off somewhere spinning his own tires and dreaming of the new Packard that in only a few weeks would be his.

And that morning, and that afternoon, as Rex might have phrased it, were the first day.

And the second day would be pretty much like the first, and the next day much the same, except that several more workers would have been hired, two of them joining Rex and me, our number of wheelbarrows and shovels doubled, while two or three of the others, these wearing hard hats and blue carpenter overalls, would be on the ground level sawing and hammering and improvising boardwalks most of which led maybe about fifty or sixty feet from the crater to a railroad sidetrack. On Thursday some additional workers appeared, these also wearing carpenter overalls with hammers in the side loops and yellow fold-up measuring rules in those slim pockets intended, I always thought, for pliers. From the bottom of the crater Rex and I and our two accomplices could see only heads and hard hats coming and going, weaving and bobbing, until with our half loads we pissanted our barrows up the incline on our journey to the familiar elm, at which times we witnessed the new workers attired in their full regalia, from their hard hats to their steel-toed boots, hustling about as if they knew precisely what the hell they were doing.

Then on Friday morning, to my amazement, Grady singled me out before I could make my first move toward my beloved wheelbarrow at the bottom of the crater.

You, he said, meaning me, I want you to build us a sawhorse. Think you can build us a sawhorse?

I said yes, I suppose I could.

Good, Grady said. The lumber is over there. He pointed. The tools and the nails are over there. He pointed again.

Rex looked at me and shrugged. I tried to grin. I knew what a sawhorse was, but I had never had the privilege of building one. With the help of my little brother I had assembled a large wooden bin that somehow had failed to dispense coal when its door was forced upon, so I knew a hammer from a handsaw. And I could envision a sawhorse because my grandfather had one in his garage, and my mother had employed a couple of them to support a large rectangle of plywood she used as a table when once in a while she and some neighbor ladies pasted and hung wallpaper. But until now I had never considered constructing one.

I went first to the shed where Grady had indicated the nails and the tools would be. It was one of several small buildings that along with additional workers had appeared suddenly and in full bloom, *surprise lilies* my maternal grandmother might have called them. Yes, there were tools aplenty in the shed – and nails and screws and nuts and bolts and hinges and you name it, and when I saw a carpenter's apron hanging from a nail on the wall I took it down and tied it around me and put nails of varying sizes into three of its pockets, then selecting what looked to be a new clawhammer and a handsaw that appeared equally pristine I left the shed almost convinced that I knew the hell what in a few minutes I'd be doing.

From a stack of lumber, the one Grady had pointed to, I grabbed some two-by-fours, a couple of two-by-sixes and several lengths of one-by-fours. I found an open spot well away from where I knew the ground-level activity would be the highest, and there I began assembling a sawhorse.

It is said that a carpenter is no better than his tools, that a chief is no bigger than his blanket. And certainly it is true that a carpenter's apron filled with newly resined nails, and a hammer and a saw that gleam their newness, provide a large measure of confidence. When my brother and I built our infamous coal bin we had to beg or borrow practically everything – or search out those items we owned but couldn't immediately find. Who hid the hammer? In which old coffee can are the assorted nails? Is there a board here, or anywhere, that isn't split from one end to the other?

So it is not surprising that I began my task with confidence. New hammer. New handsaw. New lengths of lumber. And plenty of nails.

Everything but a blueprint, and something beyond guesswork to measure with. There was no tape, no yardstick, no fold-up rule in the shed, not that I could find, anyway, so I resorted to guesswork and approximation, deciding first that the sawhorse should be as high as my waist, deciding next upon what I thought should be the angle of each leg from the top of the horse to the ground, determining thereafter how the legs might be steadied after they had been appropriately spread. All of this I more or less calculated mentally before I lifted the first board to make the first cut and, when the time arrived to make that cut I had nothing to lay the board on – certainly not a sawhorse, which at that moment would have been useful. So I stacked the boards, all but the one I intended to saw and, using the stack as a table I went to my knees to make the initial cut.

Jot this down: A truly sharp saw is an instrument not to be lightly appreciated – or regarded. You should respect if not indeed worship its well-honed, offset teeth, and you should begin your cut slowly, using the thumb on your left hand to guide the blade. I did neither, which is perhaps the reason the blade jumped, cutting a small kerf at the base of my left index finger. Have I mentioned that I was a boy scout who knew not only the oath and the pledge but also all seven of the pressure points? Fortunately, however, the cut was shallow, and the intrepid scout was able to stanch its flow easily enough by pressing his bloody finger against the left leg of his blue jeans.

I had reckoned that the job would take one hour, at the most two, or, if I ran into some unforeseeable snags, two point five. But it took almost three, counting a fifteen minute break that began at ten, Grady having instituted the break two days earlier when perhaps he noticed that the boys down in the pit, those tiny aliens, those lowly pismires, those pitiful subalterns, were moving their wheelbarrows at speeds suggesting utter fatigue. So after the break I put the finishing touches on the project, and at approximately eleven o'clock the sawhorse stood finished, whereupon I looked at it and touched it here and there and finally, for the supreme test, sat on its two-by-six top and boy howdy it passed the test, although it wobbled a bit, one of the four legs being a bit shorter than its fellows.

I didn't know what to do with it so, at length, having returned the tools and the carpenter's apron to their appropriate places, I carried it to the building Rex and I had designated as company headquarters and left it near the door, Grady being nowhere in sight. By eleven fifteen I was standing at the base of the crater shoveling dirt into my wheelbarrow, urging it one half load at a time up the incline to unload it near where the piss elum used to be, because one of the workmen, no doubt following orders, had cut it down.

During the noon hour, as we ate our sandwiches under the sprawling branches of the three maples in Zenda's city park, I told Rex, in some detail, how to put together a sawhorse, and he responded by telling me that he was reasonably certain now that he was in love with Corrinne, so that problem, he said, was pretty much solved. But another problem, he said, was a direct consequence, or at least a possible consequence, of the solving of the first problem, which was this: He feared that he might love Corrinne too much. That is, he was afraid that his love for her might diminish his love of the Lord, a love, he said in so many words, that must remain always and forever both foremost and unassailable. He might receive the call to be a missionary, for example, to travel to some remote and possibly dangerous country, and he feared that his love for Corrinne might cause him to balk, perhaps cause him to deny the call, a call that of course would be divine, in favor of his love of Corrinne, which was worldly. You know, Bill, he said, passion is a very strong human emotion, and we should never permit it to interfere with our calling.

I told him that having finished building the sawhorse I placed it near the door of company headquarters. Grady wasn't at home, I said, so I just left it there by the door.

Though I do honestly believe, Rex said, that I have the strength of character not to love Corrinne more than I love the Lord.

Rex was eating a very thick baloney sandwich. Mine was roast beef. Edna Hatfield had prepared it the evening before and had placed it in the refrigerator for me.

What do you suppose Grady is going to do with my sawhorse? And why do you suppose he chose me to build it?

The Scriptures tell us, Rex said, that we should not place anything or anyone above our God, not even the woman we marry. So what if I marry Corrinne and become so involved with her, if you know what I mean, that I refuse to endanger her life by taking her to do the Lord's work in some remote and dangerous country?

I'll be honest with you, Rex. My goddamn sawhorse was not perfect. When I sat on it, it wobbled.

But I do love her, Rex said. He was chewing the final bite of his baloney sandwich. I mean, I love her very much. I discovered late last night that I truly love her.

I believe that Grady called *me* to build the sawhorse, I said, because I look more like a carpenter than you do. More Christlike, Rex. My hands are larger and less lily white.

I held forth my left hand to exhibit not only its roughness but also its wounded index finger, its bloody kerf already beginning to heal.

Late last night, Rex said, as I was about to go to sleep, I heard a song on the radio that told me how much I love Corrinne.

I have a portable Philco, I said. I bought it when I was delivering the *Wichita Beacon*. I made payments. When I went into the store, you know, Lew's Variety, to make the final payment, Mr. Lew wouldn't take my money. He gave me the radio but wouldn't take my money. You know why?

The song was "My Happiness," Rex said. He was finished with the baloney sandwich and was washing down some gingersnaps with an Orange Crush. And the song told me how much I love Corrinne, he said, and he sang the opening lines slowly and woefully, an old story of sadness, weariness, and longing. For a moment or two I was tempted to join him, to make a duet of it. But I wasn't sure of the words — and, too, I was afraid that my basso profundo might not do much to complement the lilt of my colleague's lovely intonations.

Mr. Lew wouldn't take my money, I said, because earlier in the day my mother went into the store and made that final payment for me. You know why she did this?

I honestly believe, Rex said, that the Lord was speaking to me through the words of that song. The song is sort of a parable, if you see what I mean.

She made the final payment, I said, because my birthday was only a week or so away, and she made the final payment as a birthday gift.

I helped myself to some of Rex's gingersnaps. I was drinking a Coke.

Jesus often spoke through parables, Rex said. He would tell a story, and the story was intended to convey a message. Isn't it possible that a song might convey a message also?

So there I stood, a portable radio in one hand, and some crumpled bills in the other. Bills that I could put into my pocket to spend later on on whatever I pleased.

The Lord works in mysterious ways, Rex said, His wonders to perform. Do you know the song I'm talking about? *How I long to be with you – my happiness!*

I almost cried, I said, not entirely because I now owned a new Philco portable radio, but because my mother had dipped into savings she didn't really have to make that final payment.

Now Rex began to hum, then to sing, very softly but nonetheless very intensely. I knew the tune, so in spite of my reluctance I joined in, but only humming, hoping my low-down voice, however subdued, would heighten rather than diminish his song. Question: What rhymes with *miss?* Answer: *Kiss.* And what rhymes – almost – with *reminisce?* You guessed it: *Happiness!*

Rex Anspaugh looked a lot like a young Frank Sinatra – thin, almost to gauntness, handsome to the edge of cuteness, clean-cut and boyish – and to some extent his singing sounded like Frank Sinatra, too, his range from tenor to baritone never seeming forced. Whatever he sang he sang with a guarded intensity that gave the song a distinctive intimacy, as if he were intoning not to a public congregation, however large or small, but to the one highlighted by the lyrics – the woman in "My Happiness," for example, or Jesus in "In the Garden":

> And he walks with me, and he talks with me,
> and he tells me I am his own . . .

I had heard Rex sing that song many times, both in church and behind the wheel of his Ford, and always he sang it with a sincerity and a quiet intensity so profound that I was almost inclined to believe him. And at irregular intervals he tilted his head back ever so slightly and closed his eyes as he sang, which augmented the intimacy – and when he was behind the wheel of his Ford increased my fear that one of these times we were going to find ourselves not in the garden with Jesus but in the ditch with the Grim Reaper.

And another thing, Rex said, having finished "My Happiness," is that Corrinne's mother might be a problem. She likes me, I know, but she doesn't want Corrinne to leave home, which I can understand. Corrinne is all that she has.

I loved that radio, I said. I still do. I listen to Dave Wilson on KFH out of Wichita. He does baseball games. I like the Dodgers. Pee Wee Reese, especially. And Jackie Robinson. You like the Dodgers?

Corrinne's mother, at heart, is a fine Christian woman. Corrinne's a lot like her. Not exactly two peas in a pod, but they do have a lot in common.

Dave Wilson isn't actually watching the game he's reporting. Someone, or some machine, feeds him the information, and he takes it from there. He makes up all of the details – you know, the weight of the bat, the stance of the batter, the motion of the pitcher, the movement of the outfielder as he positions himself to catch a popup or a long fly ball. All that stuff. He makes it up. But he's damn good. He makes you think he's at the game. There's crowd noise on a record and something thwacked against something else to sound like a bat making contact with a ball. It's fantastic.

Things will work out, Rex said. I have faith, and faith is the victory. Faith, said Rex, as if he were pronouncing not only a truth but a benediction, can move mountains.

I reached for the last of the gingersnaps.

Yes, I said, but faith is not going to load our wheelbarrows and push them up that god-awful slope and dump their dirt near where the piss elum used to be. Is it?

Rex nodded, but not in response to my question. He was instead agreeing with his benediction. So totally was he in agreement with himself that he repeated it: Faith can move mountains.

Maybe on the way back to our wheelbarrows you'll want to take a look at my sawhorse, I said. I left it near the door of company headquarters.

And suddenly it occurred to me that today was Friday, that at five o'clock we could collect our first paycheck. I mentioned this to Rex.

His bright eyes brightened further. Holy shit, he said. Let's get back to work!

The figures on our paychecks were massive. Rex and I, in absolute harmony, gasped. Then, as if to confirm our amazement, Rex said it again: Holy shit!

And miracle of miracles he drove the twenty miles from Zenda to our hometown without once speaking of Corrinne, nor did he at any point along the way burst softly into song. Instead, we spoke of our work, of our wheelbarrows half filled with dirt, of our aching backs and of the several blisters on our gloveless hands, of the joy and satisfaction of having finished one full week of employment, of our monstrous paychecks, of what we might do with them, of collecting additional checks and of what we might do with these, Rex all the while driving too fast over the gravel roads, gravel like a perverse rainfall pelting the underside of the Ford, field after field of ripening wheat whizzing by, Rex and I drunk as lords on paychecks and the thought of an impending work-free weekend.

Earlier, however, when we had stood in line to receive our checks, I noticed that my sawhorse was nowhere to be seen. It was not sitting by the door of company headquarters, where I had left it, and when I turned this way and that, attempting to catch a glimpse of it, I could see nothing that remotely resembled a sawhorse.

Maybe you didn't really build one, Rex had suggested. Maybe that sawhorse is all in your ugly little head. He was feeling good, anticipating the paycheck.

Maybe your ass is grass, I said, and maybe I'm a lawnmower. I felt pretty good, too.

But the sawhorse was gone, and would remain gone, and I would never learn what happened to it; and its disappearance would make it, in memory, an icon to be revered if not worshipped, and thinking of it I would be reminded of what my friend Rex might call "The Parable of the Purloined Candy."

And there was in that country a boy and his older sister, and one December they were coerced, or maybe bribed, into singing "Star of the East" at the Christmas Eve program at their church, a thoroughly painful experience because both were shy and neither could carry a tune in a washtub. But it came to pass that they sang the song anyway, high notes and low notes and a confusion of notes in between, and behold eventually the misery came to an end and with it their reward: Santa Claus, who came ho-ho-ho-ing down the aisle, giving each eager child a sack of candy, and the boy received his candy and did not eat it, as did his older sister, she plunging a hand into her sack as if she were famished, he choosing instead to save his candy, to hide it in a secret place on the back porch at his home. And when he went to that secret place the following morning to retrieve it, behold, it was gone, the screen door open and flapping, and the boy never saw his sack of candy again, and the boy, having wept,

159

grew into manhood and into the twilight of his allotted years secure in the arms of consolation: Because the candy had disappeared without ever having been tasted, its sweetness would last forever.

When I showed my paycheck to Mother she told me to get to the bank the first thing in the morning, young man, and open a checking account. She spoke to me as if talking to a child, and like a child I obeyed her – and, having obeyed, I felt enormously mature and self-sufficient. Christ on a crutch, Rex, I said the following Monday morning as we drove to work, I have money in the bank, and a book of blank checks to spend the money with. Rex, driving much too fast, nodded and grinned.

9

Chaos often breeds life, when order breeds habit.
　　—Henry Adams, *The Education of Henry Adams*

Come, my friends,
'Tis not too late to seek a newer world.
Push off, and sitting well in order smite
The sounding furrows . . .
　　　　　　　　　—Tennyson, "Ulysses"

Money, which represents the prose of life, and which
is hardly spoken of in parlors without an apology, is,
in its effects and laws, as beautiful as roses.
　　—Ralph Waldo Emerson, *Essays: Second Series*

In the beginning was chaos, wrote the ancient Greeks, and chaos in its own sweet time gave birth to night and death . . .

I stood patiently in the midst of chaos, or near chaos, counting my blessings as I waited in line to be given a card that would ensure me a space in Fundamentals of Speech. I had no idea what Fundamentals of Speech might entail, did not know an epiglottal from an aspirate, would not recognize a phoneme should it jump up and bite me squarely on the larynx. But I was willing to stand in line if that's what it took to find out.

Patiently I stood in several lines that morning, zigzagged my way through chaos as I collected cards for all my classes – Fundamentals of Speech, biology (one card for the lecture, another for the lab), and Beginning French. I already had the card that Professor Banks had given me for Freshman Composition. It was almost noon when I left the old gymnasium, cards held tightly, to make my way to the bookstore.

Here I was, then, a man of some means – money in the bank, a couple of blank checks in my billfold. I had spent a portion of my summer earnings on a 1938 Chevrolet with a faulty clutch, a part that would fail when I attempted to drive the car across a mere hundred yards of railroad ties; and I had spent some money on room rent, enough to see me through the fall semester. In a few minutes I would stand in line at the campus center to pay for a stack of books, and I would write another check to cover my tuition. But I had money in the bank, and though it would evaporate more rapidly than I could have imagined I nonetheless at the moment was a man of considerable means.

And all of this bounty was mine because each Friday afternoon

Rex and I had been given paychecks that each time had caused us to inhale both deeply and gratefully. Our first check had given our resolve a boost and, when we returned to work the following Monday morning we already were anticipating Friday afternoon.

We had returned that morning to find the building site abuzz with men and machinery – trucks and graders and earthmovers everywhere. It was as if the preceding week had been a rehearsal for a long-running drama, and Rex and I agreed that all of our shoveling and pissanting had been a part of that rehearsal. Grady, we realized, had been testing us, had wanted to learn whether we were men enough to do the job – or did we have shit down our necks? Down at the bottom of the crater where we had broken our backs shoveling dirt into wheelbarrows was a Caterpillar with a front loader moving more earth in a minute than we had moved in half a day. On the ground level a dump truck was leaving its load of sand not far from some mixers that eventually would be delivering concrete into wheelbarrows that Rex and I and several others would guide to forms that would shape the underground walls of the elevator.

We had been met by a small wiry Irishman who called himself Speck because, he said, that's what everyone else called him because, he said, he wasn't much bigger than a speck. Understand? But don't let size fool you; it's not the size of the dog in the fight, it's the size of the fight in the dog. Now, he said, I'm the on-the-job foreman, and after you two have gotten rid of those idiotic ball caps I want you to find yourselves a couple of hard hats – then I'll show you what to do. Now go take a look in that shed over there, he said.

We found two yellow hard hats in that shed over there, left our idiotic ball caps in Rex's Ford, and located Speck. He too wore a yellow hard hat and, because it was much too small it rode high on his round Irish head, perhaps to make its wearer appear larger, at least taller, than a speck. He told us what he wanted us to do: Take those two wheelbarrows over there, he said, and start unloading the sacks of cement that you'll find in that open boxcar over there. I want you to stack those sacks between the mixers and that mound of sand. Understand?

Each morning Speck met us and gave us instructions, and each morning we followed them. Mostly we moved heavy objects from one place to another, sacks of dead weight from a boxcar to the space between the mixers and that enormous mound of sand; lumber from a different boxcar to where carpenters with their mouths full of nails were hammering together forms of various heights and shapes; and reinforcement rods from the back of a truck to wherever Speck pointed a finger. Each noon we drove to the village park to eat sandwiches and apples and drink our Coke and Orange Crush, and to enjoy a breeze, if such a thing existed, as we sat in the shade of the sprawling maples. And it got even better when another option turned up. One noon, as we were driving to the park, we noticed to our amazement that the cafe was open for business. Hot beef sandwiches and slices of apple pie almost on a par with Edna Hatfield's. And iced tea. And back to work feeling reborn.

With Speck's permission we removed our shirts and, when the foreman was out of sight, our hard hats, permitting the sun to burn our faces and bellies and backs, after which, the blisters having broken and healed, we began to tan, darkening surely and smoothly until by the time the forms were in place, ready to receive the concrete, the skin color was somewhere between acorn and ebony.

My girlfriend says I look like a Roman god, I tell Rex. We are in the shade of the maples, eating beef and baloney. She likes to press her palms against my bare back because, she says, my flesh feels warm as a kitten.

Corrinne isn't speaking to me, Rex says. I don't know why. Probably her mother.

It is near the end of June and the pouring of concrete has begun, which means that a detachment of workers must be on the job every minute of the day and night to keep the concrete flowing and the forms by means of turnable jacks rising. It is truly a large and complex operation, one that neither Rex nor I can fathom. We simply do whatever Speck, our little leprechaun, tells us to do, and inch by inch the forms ascend, leaving beneath them roundings of concrete walls that even before they are completely dry look as if they had been standing since the beginning of time. We take our turns at the jacks, rotating each handle ninety degrees as we walk the platform from one side to the other. We take our turns over the noon hours, and at night, and over a couple of weekends.

Patience. Rabelais it was, I believe, who wrote that he who has patience can surpass anything, and who among us, rotating the handles of three or four dozen jacks that in turn lift forms so slowly that progress is very difficult to discern, would care to disagree? Each morning, returning to work, Rex and I note the undeniable fruits of patience: Inch by improbable inch the concrete walls of the Zenda elevator rise in the general direction of heaven.

And night and death, wrote the ancient Greeks, gave birth to love, and love in and of itself created light and day, and these two, cohabiting, brought forth the earth, female who gave birth to her husband, the heavens . . .

Patiently I waited in line to pay for an assortment of books and for a light to place atop the small desk in the wide narrow sunroom I shared with my hometown buddies, Toar and Gene. The woman at the cash register smiled when she told me how much I owed her – a lot more than I expected. I tried to smile back. I fumbled for my billfold, removed a blank check and asked for a pen. That morning I had enjoyed a breakfast of scrambled eggs and toast and a large glass of tomato juice in the college cafeteria, where I saw a help-wanted sign. As I handed the check to the woman at the cash register, mentally recording this sudden large drain on my checking account, I decided to apply for the job.

One early afternoon Rex, beside me turning handles, said that the building of an elevator must be a lot like the building of the tower of Babel.

I didn't disagree, because our turning of the jack handles, and the nonstop feeding of concrete into the wooden forms, had lifted the walls of the elevator almost into the clouds, one of which was directly overhead and so near that with a broomstick I might have reached it. But it was my understanding that the Zenda elevator was not meant to be a staircase to paradise but instead was intended to house upwards of half a million bushels of Kingman County grain. That's what the sign near company headquarters claimed, anyway.

I have never enjoyed heights – those heights, that is, that provide no barrier between me and the edge of whatever I am standing on. Rex and I were on a platform made of two-by-sixes, moving from one side to the other, east to west, then back, west to east, moving slowly and just as slowly turning the handles on the jacks, and there was nothing, no wire, no wall, no anything, to prevent us from stepping off the edge and falling a long, long distance to our certain deaths. I had no intention of walking off, of course, but when I turned the jack nearest the edge, and looked down, I felt a giddy disorientation that made me unsure of where my next step might take me. Sometimes, though – safely away from the edge – I'd feel an exhilaration that prompted me to hum or to sing or to whistle, and more often than not Rex would join in, singing lines from a hymn while I sang lines from a country western, Jesus and cowhand as if lion and lamb lying down peacefully, though a trifle discordantly, together. Henry David Thoreau, at Walden Pond, wrote that *Heaven is under our feet as well as over our heads*, and during those hours I spent on the platform turning handles, in my small way creating the walls of the Zenda, Kansas, elevator, I felt that heaven must be that place where both earth and sky could be viewed from a vantage point suspended somehow between them. This would make heaven not just one place, but instead a joining of places from which everything can be acknowledged, perceived, appreciated, loved. I looked down, far down, to see a crisscrossing of human figures doing whatever Speck asked or de-manded – the mixing of concrete, the hauling of it then to the bucket that the crane with its cable would lift to those workers at the perilous edge of the platform, workers who in their deter-mined, inscrutable ways would guide the mixture into the maws of the forms. I looked up, far up, to see a blueness made bluer by white bursts of cumulus, or an explosion of scattered birds on their way to – where? To a pond, maybe, or to nests from which they might look up and down to perceive, in their own birdlike ways, the nature of heaven.

And earth and the heavens gave birth to the immortals, wrote the ancient Greeks, begat at least two races before they birthed the Titans, who would rule for untold ages . . .

In the kitchen at the college cafeteria I stood feeding dirty dishes into a tunnel of steam. Bill Johnson, an upperclassman who had spent perhaps five minutes teaching me the tricks of the trade, stood beside me. Johnson was a handsome young black student whose abundance of energy both wearied and impressed me. I had never known a black person; in fact, the only minority in my town was Joe Mora, that good silent man I'd come to admire when in less than a year I'd work with him on the railroad. And my town had been pretty much free of Catholics, too, only a couple of families having successfully infiltrated the protestant ranks. I had watched some black actors and actresses on the screen at the Rialto, and the Plainview Cardinals had two black players in their backfield when the Bulldogs took their measure in Wichita, but otherwise my knowledge of anyone not of my own color and theology was scant if not nonexistent.

Ah, but Bill Johnson was the ideal young man to remove whatever walls might exist between one individual and another. His spirit was infectious. He taught me how to feed the dirty dishes into the steamer, then stood aside and watched to make certain that I did it right. He observed me for most of the morning, correcting me only once or twice, watched until Miss Bishop, the tall, lean, tight-lipped woman who had hired me with a swiftness that only Grady could have matched, walked into the room and Bill, suddenly deciding that I could handle the job on my own, went to the far side of the steam tunnel and joined another employee in the removing and drying of the squeaky-clean dishes.

Capable and bright, Bill Johnson also could yodel, and he did it without fanfare, without tilting his head back and without making a megaphone of his hands to send the sounds all the way to kingdom come. No, he simply intoned his yodel as if he were my buddy Rex singing a hymn or swatches of "My Happiness," yodeling easily as he went about his work or as he supervised my activities. I was so impressed with his yodeling that I began to imitate him and, because I did a pretty fair job of it he was likewise impressed – with himself as a mentor, I believe, and with me as his protégé. What I did not tell him was that I had spent a lot of time listening to the likes of "Texas" Jim Robertson on the jukebox at my parents' cafe, had also spent many hours in the Rialto watching and listening to such stalwart cowpokes as Roy Rogers and Gene Autry as they rode off into their glowing sunsets, always yodeling, and because I loved and envied them I tried, in the privacy of, say, the barn or the outhouse, to sound like them, attempted to cultivate a falsetto I could move into and out of without completely destroying my vocal chords.

Our yodeling was not extremely loud, but it had to rise way above a whisper if we were to be heard at all. There was a lot of noisy activity in the cafeteria facility, women in an adjoining room cooking everything from soup to nuts, student employees delivering trays of that same soup and nuts – and ham loaf, ham loaf, ham loaf – to the serving line as other workers returned empty trays to me or whoever was on duty at the steamer, the steamer gurgling and hissing, silverware jingling, and dishes clattering. And in the midst of all this clamor and bustle Bill Johnson and his understudy yodeled gleefully as they worked, perhaps appearing for all the world like two young men who had the world by its tail and could bring it down, if they wanted to, with a single pull.

I sat with Rex in the shade of our maples holding a sandwich in one hand and removing sweat from my Romanesque torso with a napkin I held in the other.

What I did not know on this particular day, a Wednesday, was that before the end of the month I will have purchased a 1938 Chevrolet and, urged on by my friend Jimmy I'll put my Chevy to the test on the rails of the Atchison, Topeka, and Santa Fe – a test that the Chevy's clutch will fail to pass.

What I did know on that Wednesday was that in three days I would turn eighteen.

I mentioned this to Rex.

Yes, he said, and would you believe it? Corrinne's birthday is coming up this month also.

Is she speaking to you now? I asked. I had difficulty keeping track of who was speaking, or not speaking, to whom.

Yes, said Rex. And would you believe it? Her mother has changed her mind about me. Corrinne says she thinks her mother now would actually bless our union.

I said, Holy shit.

We finished our meal, secured our lunch buckets and drove back to the work site where our elevator had risen as high as its blueprints allowed. Rex parked his Ford just a few feet east of company headquarters. As we got out of the car and were looking for Speck, who would tell us what our jobs for the afternoon would be, we were approached by Grady. He held two white envelopes in his right hand.

You boys are late, he said.

We responded by looking at our watches. We were not late. We were five minutes early.

I don't like it when my workers take more than one hour to eat their lunch, Grady said. You're fired.

I looked at Rex, who was looking at me. I wanted to say, We are not late. But I didn't. Neither did Rex.

Here, Grady said.

He gave each of us a white envelope, then offered his hand. I shook it. Rex did the same. I started to say something, but before the first word could be spoken Grady was gone.

We did not open the envelopes until we had retired our hard hats and returned to the Ford. They contained our final paychecks.

Rex looked at his and said, Holy shit. I think they gave us a bonus.

We sat there for a few minutes examining the figures. Yes, we had been given a bonus; and it took us a while to put two and two together, to reconcile the bonus with the firing, until finally we realized that we had not in fact been fired – we had been let go because there was no more work left for us to do, and Grady's method of releasing us was perfectly in keeping with his tough-as-leather image.

Well, Rex said finally, we might as well go home.

We were well on our way to Attica before we fully realized that our summer work was finished, actually and honestly and forever and ever finished, at which moment we looked at each other and let loose a whoop that must surely yet be echoing in the nonexistent arroyos of Harper County. And Rex, who was driving too fast, followed up his whoop by saying, Tonight I am going to ask Corrinne to marry me.

I didn't know what to say so I said, Holy shit.

Because now, Rex said, I'm certain it's what God wants me to do.

I didn't know what to say so I asked, Are you sure?

The smile on Rex's face suggested a peculiar blend of the beatific and the goofy. He seemed to be basking in the aftermath of an epiphany brought on no doubt by his personal relationship with God and augmented perhaps by his delight over a fat paycheck made even fatter by an unexpected bonus.

I'll drive to Anthony this afternoon, Rex said, and buy an engagement ring. It'll make the perfect birthday gift. Did I tell you that Corrinne has a birthday this month?

He did not wait for the reply I had no intention of making. Instead, he began to hum, then to sing –"My Happiness," of course, with its familiar sadness and weariness and longing.

Well, I felt pretty good myself. I too had a big paycheck that sported a bonus. I too had a girlfriend that I intended to impress, though not with an engagement ring. We might go to a movie, or more likely settle for a drive in the country, if the family vehicle wasn't tied up. It was going to be a pleasant evening, you could see that much already – a long pleasant evening in August, your summer work behind you, your final paycheck deposited in your account, your bronze, godlike body showered and smelling of Lifebuoy and, only three short days away, your official entry into manhood: your eighteenth birthday.

And the immortals, the Titans, created man and woman, wrote the ancient Greeks, created them in the image of the reigning gods because these at last had been created in the image of those lovely mythmaking mortals who created them . . .

My first college class met at eight in the morning on the fourth floor of the huge administration building. Freshman Composition. With me I carried two texts, John M. Kierzek's *The Macmillan Handbook of English*, and *A Quarto of Modern Literature*, edited by Leonard Brown and Porter G. Perrin. The latter was a large book, large enough to have been a blood relative of the *Lincoln Library of Essential Information*. It was composed of short stories, plays, and poems as well as biographies, historical pieces, and some factual prose.

The hallways in the ad building were wide and endless – and full of smoke. I seemed to be the only student not holding a cigarette, which made me feel both inadequate and out of place. I had tried my hand at smoking, had taken cigarettes from my parents' filling station and cafe, and had also sneaked a few cigarettes when I rolled them for my father on a contraption he bought one day from a salesman whose rounds often brought him to our cafe.

When I was in grade school I smoked Folgers coffee rolled in toilet paper – or tried to. I'd sit outside with my buddy R. D., our shoulder blades against the back wall of the Rialto, and we'd roll some coffee into a length of toilet paper, strike a kitchen match and light up, behind us the sounds of a Saturday night western trembling the wall. But the smoke from Folgers coffee is difficult to love, especially when it is inhaled, and maybe the taste of that experience was still with me when I snitched a pack of Camels or Lucky Strikes from my parents' places of business. In any case, I was a failed smoker, and I had to confront my shortcoming as I walked down the smoke-filled hallway in the general direction of the room where my class in Freshman Composition was scheduled to begin. (I should mention that only our professors were permitted to smoke in the classrooms, which meant that a student who smoked had to do so in the hallways and – so it seemed – tried to smoke enough to survive until the class ended.)

There were stout wooden benches lining the walls of the hallway, each with an ashtray at the end of an armrest, and many students were sitting there, all of them, I thought, smoking, some with books on their laps, others with books balanced on the armrests, others with no books at all. Everyone seemed to know everyone else. They were talking and laughing and blowing smoke and flicking ashes that most often missed the trays.

Feeling altogether out of place among the hallway crowd, I went into the classroom whose number matched the one on my admittance card. I was the only one there. I was not only not late, I was more than early. I found a desk at the end of the third row near a window, its top engraved with graffiti, which I covered with my *Quarto*. Through the open door at my right I could see and hear my fellow students as they milled about in the hallway. Finally, one of them came into the room, followed by another, then another, and I, wanting to appear studious, opened my Macmillan hand-book to learn that one should use a plural verb with a compound subject joined by *and*: A *horse* and a *cow are* in the pasture. And a pig and a hog and a cow were in the cow lot, too, that day my brother and I went swimming in a sea of ooze, the knot that se-cured the swing to the rope having come untied and, sitting in a desk chair in a college classroom early that morning I could yet smell that distinctive blend of mud and manure, could yet hear my brother laughing like a little moron as he prepared to dive back into the muck, could feel the cold water from the garden hose . . .

A *boy* and his *brother were* in the cow lot.

When the professor entered, the students hushed. He was slim and square-faced and was wearing a dark blue suit and a light blue tie. He was handsome. He was not smoking. He was carrying two books, which he placed on a desk at the front of the room. He looked at all of us as if looking at each of us. He smiled. He said softly, Hello. He said, My name is Loy Banks. He said, Welcome to Freshman Composition.

10

When the cup that is full is added to, the cup runs over.

—Kansas lore

If I should certainly say to a novice, "Write from experience and experience only," I should feel that this was rather a tantalizing monition if I were not careful immediately to add, "Try to be one of the people on whom nothing is lost."

—Henry James, "The Art of Fiction"

Into the face of the young man who sat on the terrace of the Hotel Magnifique at Cannes there had crept a look of furtive shame, the shifty, hang-dog look which announces that an Englishman is about to talk French.

—P. G. Wodehouse, *The Luck of the Bodkins*

Overflow. It's what exists when something liquid flows over something that isn't liquid – wine over the brim of a goblet, for example, or water over a dip in a gravel road.

The dip in the gravel road one mile north of town was covered with concrete to keep the stream from washing away the gravel and thus the road. Everyone called this "the overflow," and of course its name became most meaningful when it flowed over, which it did after a rainfall – if the rainfall were significantly more than a drizzle. It was a place my brother and I loved to hike to and wade in, when we weren't in school and when our parents were not at home to deny us permission. And it was the place my father had in mind one Sunday afternoon when in a frisky mood he told me to jump into the family jalopy because, he said, I am going to take you for a little ride.

I was dumbfounded. This was not something my father did very often because almost always he was working, if not at a job away from home then at a job at home, and very rarely were he and I alone together. Where was my brother? My sister? My mother?

I jumped into the family jalopy, a Ford Model-A, and Father, already behind the wheel, quickly found reverse and in a matter of seconds we had cleared the driveway and Father deftly shifted into low gear and released the clutch and we were off. Had it not rained all morning we would have left a cloud of dust as we headed west to a nearby intersection where we sped around the corner and headed due north.

Thanks to a mixture of sand and gravel the road was not sloppy. The rain had stopped a couple of hours ago and, though we could see a few clouds to the north and east there did not seem to be any threat of additional rain. The sun was shining. The windows were down. Father at the wheel was grinning. At his right his son sat rigid as stone, inhaling everything.

One mile north of town Father turned east and headed toward the dip in the road that would mean *overflow* – and indeed that's precisely what it was, the dip with its concrete bottom flooded with moving water. I could not see exactly how deep the overflow was, but I was about to find out – because Father to my absolute amazement did not stop the Model-A as it approached the flow; instead, he shifted to low and eased the vehicle forward until the front wheels touched the moving water, then continued until the water very nearly reached the running-board, and he did not brake to a stop until we were sitting at the bottom of the dip, a motorized vessel aground in an unlikely sea.

Father looked at me and laughed; perhaps he had noticed that I was more bewildered than entertained, and he wanted me to relax, to know that everything was under control. He opened his door and turning sideways removed his low-topped boots and his socks, then rolled the legs of his overalls up past his knees. I did the same, though I had not yet opened my door.

I was awed by the rushing water. On several occasions my brother and I had been to the overflow to watch the water trickle across the road and to launch boats in the form of sticks all the way, we supposed, to the ocean. But this was different. The water was considerably more than a trickle, for one thing, higher and faster than I had ever seen it, and for another there was something unnatural, or so it seemed, about parking the family Ford in the channel of a river, however confined or temporary that stream might be.

From the backseat Father retrieved a tin dipper, the one normally kept near the reservoir attached to the kitchen range, then he confidently stepped into the current and made his way to the driver's side of the hood, which he unlatched and folded back. I had crawled across the seat and entered the water and was standing now at Father's right, watching him and wondering what next he might be up to.

What he was up to was replenishing the cells of the battery with rainwater because, he'll tell me, rainwater is soft water, and soft water is best for the battery. Although Father was not a mechanic, what little he knew about automobiles he knew absolutely, and in this instance he knew that soft water is best for the battery. Absolutely.

I watched him remove the caps from the cells, slowly and deliberately, as if performing a ritual. Watched him bend over to fill the tin dipper from the flow of soft rushing water. Watched him pour the water into the cells, being careful not to overfill them because, he'll tell me later, overfilled cells will shorten the life of the battery. Watched him replace the caps. Watched him lower and relatch the hood.

Watched him fill the dipper again. Watched him lift the dipper to his mouth and drink.

It is not possible to describe this scene clearly enough – not the blue sky with its scattering of spent clouds to the north and east, or the meadowlark I probably saw perched on a willow limb that reached halfway across the rushing water, or the rushing water itself, or the small red plane whose steady baritone I heard before I saw the plane – or, most especially, this: my father in blue overalls with their legs rolled up almost to the knees standing hatless in the middle of a rushing stream drinking rainwater from a tin dipper. And this: my father bending over to refill the dipper to offer it to his son who will balk, but only briefly, before taking the dipper and looking into it to see the cool, clear water, who will close his eyes to drink from the dipper, who will open his eyes to see his father smiling . . .

How long did we stand there, my father and I, in water rushing hell-bent to the ocean? Not very long, I suppose, though it seemed a long time, perhaps because the water against my legs was so relentless, and I remember thinking that if I am swept away the car will be swept away also, because I was standing upstream beside it, and my fear in its own obtuse way no doubt heightened my pleasure and I was therefore determined to remain knee-deep in the rushing water until my father told me to get back into the car, which at last he did.

And he did too, and we sat there without saying anything for a minute or so, our boots and shoes and socks on the floorboard, the tin dipper returned to the back seat.

Well, Father said after he had started the car, that should just about do it.

I nodded. I said, That should just about do it.

Father found low gear and the Model-A, shivering slightly, moved slowly up and out of the overflow.

Overflow. It's what exists when something liquid flows over something that isn't liquid – wine over the brim of a goblet, or water over a dip in a gravel road.

Or the feeling that happens when something you find yourself smack in the middle of can't be contained.

Professor Banks said, Welcome to Freshman Composition, and soon enough, after we had read and discussed two stories in the *Quarto*, Willa Cather's "Neighbor Rosicky" and James Joyce's "Counterparts," he gave us a writing assignment. Compose an essay that characterizes a member of your family. So I penned my first essay, wrote it and worried over it and revised it and worried some more until the deadline forced me to turn it in. It was an attempt to characterize one side of my father's difficult personality. I called it "Overflow."

Professor Banks treated the essay kindly, and I was encouraged. I therefore approached the second writing assignment with more confidence. Write an essay, said Professor Banks, in which you confront your memory of a near-death experience. By this time we had read and discussed Ernest Hemingway's "The Short Happy Life of Francis Macomber" and Shirley Jackson's "The Lottery."

I began at once to think about possible subjects for my essay. When I was about six I very nearly drowned in a spring-fed farm pond. At the last moment my father had rescued me, had pulled me from the water and pumped me dry, Mother beside him weeping and wringing her hands. When I was in the sixth grade, and delivering the *Wichita Beacon* on my bicycle, I was very nearly struck by a car I did not see because 1) the Evangelical United Brethren Church blocked my view, and 2) I did not slow down. I approached the blacktop doing ninety or so, and was half way across when I heard first a scream, then a *snick*, and looking to my left as I applied the brake I saw the back end of the car whose bumper had grazed the reflector on my rear fender. The scream had come from an elderly woman sitting in a car parked near the church, where she could see it all – the vehicle rapidly approaching from the west, and my bike, with me aboard, passing just in front of it. Wham and bam. Zip and snick. The near miss happened too quickly for me to be frightened, though I have been scared, off and on, ever since.

My brother almost bled to death when he cut an artery in the bottom of his foot while swimming in a pond east of town, cut the artery on some glass from a window of an old Hudson that lay at the bottom of the pond; and because Professor Banks said that the near-death experience could be our own or someone else's, preferably someone we were close to, I could have written about my brother's severed artery, how watching the blood come not in a stream but in spurts I realized, I believe for the first time, that mortality is not only a fact but also that it doesn't give a tinker's damn whether its victim is a complete stranger or your little brother. Happily, though, it was only a near-death experience. My brother's life was saved by an older buddy who applied pressure to the appropriate point until we got Johnny into town where Dr. Montzingo stitched him up and told him and me and our buddy, too, to be more careful the next time we were stupid enough to go swimming in a sandpit with the hulk of an old Hudson lying in wait at the bottom.

I decided finally not to write about my near drowning, or about the near miss when the bumper of a speeding car snicked the reflector on the rear fender of my bicycle, or about my brother's cut artery. I chose instead to write about the time I sparred with the rear wheel of a John Deere tractor and very nearly went down for the count.

It happened on an early Friday afternoon in August. Danny Burke had convinced me to spend the day with him on his farm less than half a mile northeast of the high school. I had to be convinced, because Danny was not one of my closest friends. He was a year older, and he was considered to be a little hell-raiser if not an outright bully. Red-haired and freckled, Danny was fearless, a trait that once in a while earned him a bloody nose, particularly when he challenged someone larger and equally fearless, which of course from time to time he did. So when I agreed to spend the afternoon at his farm I did so less out of desire than out of fear: turn him down and he might knock my block off.

Even so, I liked Danny; he had a wide, disarming smile, and I

admired his bravado when it was directed at something or someone other than me. So when he confronted his father Sanford,
who looked just like Danny, just larger and older, and insisted that
he and his friend Billy be permitted to go with Mr. Burke to the
field, and ride with him on the tractor for several rounds as he
plowed a small plot south of the house, I hoped Mr. Burke would
let us. I had been on a tractor only two or three times, all of them
at my grandfather's farm, and each time I was required to stand in
front of Grandfather as he sat on a large metal seat superintending
his lug-wheeled John Deere. And each time I was very impressed,
not only with the massiveness of the tractor as it crept over and
around the rocks that infested all of my grandfather's quarter section, but also with the process of readying the tractor for its work
– the greasing, the gassing-up, the checking of the oil and, most
especially, the handling of the flywheel to start the motor. Grandfather would move the wheel slowly until the compression, as he
called it, was precisely right, at which time he would grunt mightily as he spun the wheel counterclockwise, releasing his hands
quickly to avoid a broken wrist should the wheel suddenly reverse
itself, a phenomenon I witnessed more than once, the wheel as if
something savage kicking back; but always Grandfather remembered to remove his hands from the beast, remove them more
quickly than I thought possible, then he'd stand back and wait for
several seconds, spitting into those large, cat-quick hands, before
confronting the flywheel again.

Sanford Burke yielded. We walked across the yard to the tractor,
a John Deere much newer of course than my grandfather's, and
Mr. Burke told us how to arrange ourselves, Danny at his right,
standing, I at his left, standing also, Mr. Burke sitting in the large
metal seat. The tractor had no fenders, but we could steady ourselves, he said, by placing a hand on his shoulder.

Mr. Burke did not need to contend with a flywheel. He merely pushed a starter button while manipulating the choke and with a puff of smoke rising from a vertical exhaust pipe the engine started and the Johnny-popper popped and, with the tractor in low gear we were on our way to the field. As we moved slowly along I found it a bit difficult to keep my balance because the field, thick with wheat stubble, was uneven, uneven to the extent that I found myself clutching Mr. Burke's shoulder – that is, clutching the blue cotton shirt that covered his shoulder. And I noticed that Danny, for all his fearlessness, held tightly to the shirt on his father's other shoulder. Between us Mr. Burke sat swaying with the swaying of the tractor, all three of us swaying, but swaying gently, swaying almost in a rhythm as the John Deere in low gear crawled eastward along a fence line toward what looked to be a three-bottom plow.

What I did not know at the time was that the stage was set for a real disaster, with me as the leading character. Someone – perhaps Sanford Burke himself – had attached concrete weights to the insides of the rear wheels, and he, or someone, had secured the weights with large bolts, and apparently he, or someone, had run out of bolts of the correct length and had used one that was much longer than necessary, and when the tractor hit a chuckhole, then another, and I widened my stance to maintain my balance, this long bolt snagged my overalls and took me forward and down and under and up until the wheel stopped turning because I must have whooped or screamed and Mr. Burke must have wasted no time hitting the clutch.

What matters when you survive a sudden near-death experience is that you survive. It is really as simple as that. In less time than it takes to inhale, you are either crushed to death by a force that outweighs you by several tons, or you are not crushed, in which case you find yourself getting to your feet to see kneeling in front of you a red-haired farmer who is looking at you with eyes so sharply and deeply focused you want to ask him to tell you what in heaven's name he is looking at. At the moment you are not aware that under your overalls your skin along the left side of your body has been scraped off, or that the left half of your face has been rubbed raw, or that the taste in your mouth is that of dry south-central Kansas dirt. You are not even particularly grateful that you are alive, because to be young is to be alive, come hell or high water or a tractor's rotating tire. At the moment you are chiefly if not exclusively impressed with the unblinking intensity of Sanford Burke's eyes, intensity softened by something moist around their edges.

Nor do you object when the arms of the farmer reach for you and take you into them, or when the farmer rises and turning his back on his tractor walks in one of the tracks the John Deere made back along the fence line toward the house where he will place you as if a large doll on the counter beside the sink to wash your face more tenderly than possible with a warm blue cloth, and you will not remember where the fearless Danny was or what he might have been doing as his father cleans your face, will not remember much about your mother's brief near-panic reaction when the farmer delivers you home; but you will remember clearly and always the farmer's eyes, and the silence, no one saying anything that you can remember, just the blue washcloth in the red-haired farmer's hand laving your skin, and his eyes looking at you as if you are something too delicate to have survived, something far beyond the scope of anyone's gratitude, or understanding.

Professor Banks had said, Welcome to Freshman Composition, and I was beginning to feel that I was indeed welcome because his

187

comments on my second essay were mostly positive. He corrected two or three errors and noted where in the handbook I could find explanations for them, but for the most part he was (or so he wrote in fluid cursive at the end of the paper) impressed.

In my greenness I appreciated any encouragement, however mild, and Freshman Composition seemed by far the most likely place for me to get it. I was struggling in biology; to the professor who taught the course, and to his student assistant, I must have resembled one of the troglodytes most of the class had long since evolved away from. In one laboratory session, for example, I was given a frog to dissect, a very dead frog, and I cut it up, but was unable to identify the poor web-footed amphibian's parts. They all looked about the same to me, so I identified them more or less at random, causing the student assistant, a girl strikingly beautiful in her white lab apron, to look at me and shake her lovely head slowly, as if to say that I was a hopeless case, a primitive chunk of stonewort or moss absolutely beyond redemption.

And things were almost as bad in Beginning French, which to this day I believe was misnamed. Some of my fellow students had taken French in high school, but undoubtedly because they did not feel confident enough to try Advanced French they chose Beginning French, and the professor, Dr. Minnie M. Miller, probably assumed that all of us were in this same boat so she navigated accordingly, speaking to us in French most of the time, which meant that an unwashed novice like myself had to scramble to keep pace, had to wait to see how those who were more advanced reacted to Dr. Miller's instructions so that I could follow suit. It was frustrating, but I tried to meet the challenge with *beaucoup d'vivre*, because I knew that now I was in a real college class being taught by a bona fide professor who had a PhD and who could speak French with her eyes closed, which she frequently did, and who had written a book, *First Readings in French Literature*, which we used as one of the basic texts.

Dr. Miller was a no-nonsense professor, though she knew how to laugh, or cackle, when something struck her as amusing. She was not a young woman, but her energy and enthusiasm suggested that she could never grow old. She was tall and thin and slightly bent over, her lips narrow and pursed, her nose pretty much a beak, her eyes small and round and youthfully bright. Her face was totally free of cosmetics, and she kept her graying hair in a bun held in place with several small, curved combs. She had long arms, and her hands were impressively strong, a fact that I learned, but not without some pain, the morning Dr. Minnie M. Miller rearranged my face.

It happened early in the semester when I was awash in a sea of bilingual ignorance. I had pronounced *monsieur* incorrectly, and a shocked and dismayed Professor Miller asked me to try again, whereupon I repeated the mispronunciation, and so on. When I had exhausted what I believed to be all reasonable possibilities, Dr. Miller fixed me with her small round eyes and shaking her head – only in that one respect reminding me of the pretty assistant in my biology lab – walked briskly to where I was sitting. Then, standing beside me, between my chair and the one at my right, she covered my face with one of her wide sinewy hands and, instructing me to say the word again, and to keep saying it, slowly, she began to rearrange my face, especially the area around my mouth, her shortest finger under my chin, the other fingers kneading my flesh with a firmness that Edna Hatfield at her bread dough would surely have envied. I continued meanwhile to say *monsieur*, slowly, *muh-shoe*, *muh-shoe*, *muh-shoe*, slowly, varying the pitch from one effort into another, my humiliation somewhat diminished by the pain, *muh-shoe*, *muh-shoe*, my face at the mercy of Dr. Miller's unmerciful fingers, until *voila!* I happened upon the correct pronunciation. Partially satisfied, my professor then stopped the kneading, but she kept her grip on my face until I had repeated *monsieur* correctly at least half a dozen times, whereupon she removed her hand ever so carefully, apparently not wanting to disturb the contortions her hand had sculpted, and I continued my recitation until my humiliation was absolute and I was told to stop.

I began to fear that I would never learn to pronounce French and, perhaps influenced by what I was learning about evolution in my biology class, but in truth more likely because I was looking for an excuse, I concluded that my inability to say a word like *monsieur* was the fault of my German ancestry. To be a very nearly full-blooded German in a French class was not fair, I thought. Germans are physically incapable of saying such things as *muh-shoe* and *ouvrit les yeux* and *N'est-ce pas vous qui vous appelez Sganarelle?* No, Germans are not built for such nasal utterances. Germans want their words to begin deep in the throat and, insofar as possible, remain there. I knew this because my maternal grandmother came to this country from southern Germany, and she was square-faced and wide-lipped and she spoke from deep in the throat, as if having gargled she could not stop gargling. Professor Miller, on the other hand, was thin-faced and nasal and spoke through pinched lips that seemed always about to kiss someone, or some thing. True, Dr. Miller had not been born and raised in France, as had my grandmother in Germany, but my professor had traveled to France many times, she said, and she had compiled and edited not only *First Readings in French Literature*, but also had written a travel book that took the reader on a cultural tour of France, with a focus upon that country's art museums, especially the Louvre; so she knew France like the back of her hand, she said, which in my view made her pretty much a Frenchwoman. And certainly her physical appearance augmented her facility with the language. I am sure that in Paris she could have passed easily as a native Parisian.

In approximately thirty years I'd travel to Paris with my wife and my little brother and his wife, but the French that I had suffered a squeezed face to learn in Dr. Miller's class would fail to serve me, although I remembered the sentence, *Si vous ne relentez pas tout de suite, c'est la derniere fois que je vais avec vous.* But not even this pitiful threat helped me, because I did not have the courage to speak it, in spite of the fact that the taxi taking us from Cherbourg to Paris was moving at speeds destined to make wrecks of us all, in any language.

Ah, but the Louvre was wonderful! It surpassed even Chartre, that lovely cathedral we visited the day before — Chartre, with a blueness in its windows that no human tongue could adequately describe, though our guide, with his busy tongue, tried to. There is no blue like the blue in the windows of this cathedral, he said, and his assertion, spoken thank God in English, caused me to think of colors in *my* America that might compete with this shade of blue in *his* France, among them the green on the John Deere tractor that tried to kill me, *John Deere green* we called it, its green being that unique, and I wondered if *Chartre Cathedral blue* had earned among the French such a popular distinction.

Ah, but the Louvre. It would inspire poetry. The Louvre,

> where Mona Lisa behind a doubled wall of glass
> hangs motionless, defying gravity,
> where the backs of the gleaners
> bend forever into their harvest,

where man and woman recline together
as if unashamed,
their bodies so immediate
I touch mine.

One of the most accomplished painters of human bodies was Rubens, I believe, whose works affirmed the value and necessity, and remarkable beauty, of form. Here is the human figure, the paintings suggest, and it is abundantly attractive because it does not seem to care that in the eyes of some it isn't, its lovely nonchalance enabling it to know pure pleasure, its attitude reflecting that of the artist who with materials he has not created and is incapable of creating has nevertheless created a perception that has found something solid by which to reveal itself. And you find yourself touching yourself to determine whether you are as genuine as the figure before you.

I paddled hard in Professor Miller's class, but I was having difficulty staying afloat. Her fingers had left persistent memories on my face, which I believe helped somewhat with my pronunciation. Even so, I was struggling. I spent a lot of time, when I wasn't in the cafeteria kitchen feeding dirty dishes into the steamer and yodeling with my mentor Bill Johnson, studying the intricacies of *avoir* and *etre*, and reading one of the works in Dr. Miller's book. She had assigned me the part of Sganarelle – scenes one through three of the first act of *Le Medecin Malgre Lui* – and having finished the translating I went to work on the pronunciation which, in spite of her attempt to rearrange my face, did not satisfy my professor. She therefore one morning invited me to remain for a few minutes after class.

Your pronunciation is not very crisp, she told me.
I nodded.

You are much too deliberate in your moving from one word to another, she said.

I agreed.

Perhaps, she said, you need to spend more time in the listening room.

I neither nodded nor agreed. I did not know what she was talking about.

Our *Medecin* recordings are excellent, she said. How often have you been listening to them?

I was sitting in my chair opening and closing Dr. Miller's book. Dr. Miller stood in front of her desk with her arms crossed, but she appeared less threatening than honestly concerned.

Not very often, I said, which was close to being true, and much safer in this instance I thought than to say "not at all." Actually, the stark truth was that I did not know that a "listening room" existed. Somehow, and to this day I don't know how, I had not heard Dr. Miller or anyone else say a single word about a listening room; but I lacked the courage to admit this to my professor.

Well, said Dr. Miller, you should make it a point to visit the listening room more often – at least three times a week.

I said that I would.

I know that you are not shirking, Professor Miller said. You attend class regularly, and it is apparent that you have been doing your homework. This is especially evident in your understanding of the grammar and vocabulary.

I almost gave myself away by asking where the listening room was located, but I knew that the question would reveal the fact that I had not visited it; instead, I said that I would listen to the records more often, and I did, and though I'd finish the French class with respectability I would not finish it with any degree of excellence – I had to spend far too much time simply catching up.

Is it any wonder, then, that I so appreciated Professor Loy Banks's encouragement? Welcome to Freshman Composition, he had said when he met the class for the first time. And when I considered how things were going in biology and Beginning French, I felt fortunate – indeed blessed – to have been a member of Professor Loy Banks's composition class.

In his class I would write several more papers – an extended library paper fully documented, an analysis of a poem (William H. Auden's "Musee des Beaux Arts"), and two or three additional essays based upon personal experience, one of which I remember in particular because I wrote it soon after the paper about my near-death experience while riding Sanford Burke's John Deere tractor.

This one had a tractor in it also, another John Deere, and perhaps I chose this subject because the earlier John Deere essay had succeeded, so I thought I might as well try another. The tractor in this essay, however, did not reach out and snatch my overalls in an attempt to abbreviate my life; this one had no long bolt to do the snatching, no concrete wheel weight that required such a bolt. It was instead a friendly machine, perfectly happy it seemed to me to be pulling a three-bottom plow across a field roughly the size of Siberia. The field belonged to my buddy Ray Asper's parents, and I agreed to help with the plowing because Ray offered me the job and promised to pay me more, he said, than the job was worth.

More than the job was worth? Not hardly – because the job seemed endless, round after endless round under a July sun that wanted to make mincemeat of my skin, and would have, too, were it not for my long-sleeved shirt and a wide-brimmed straw hat that made me look like a storybook hayseed. And the monotony – round after endless round of watching stubble become soft dark earth, most of which found its way into my nostrils. To pass the time I talked to the tractor, pretending, for example, that the machine was my buddy Ray. Shouting over the rhythmic chug-chug-chug of the John Deere, I took immense pleasure in addressing my buddy as a shitbird or a dipstick or a numbnut, three of my favorite slurs. Ray Asper, you shitbird, I might say, when I finish this job and collect my paycheck I am going to destroy you. The outrageous threat would tickle me and I'd laugh out loud, and I fancied that the Johnny-popper, since it did not seem to object, was laughing also; and when I thought of an additional threat I'd voice it, too. The smears and taunts amused me because they were so ridiculous, so absolutely unfounded – because in truth I admired Ray Asper profoundly. He was an only child, the undisputed apple of his parents' eyes, and he was perhaps the most fearless fullback ever to have worn an Attica Bulldog helmet. If you want proof, ask anyone who played on defense that fall for the Plainview Cardinals, a team we will throttle in November, long after this forlorn field has been plowed and planted and forgotten. Time and again my buddy Ray will lower his helmet to plunge into and through and over those Cardinal galoots hunkered in his path. On the gridiron, time and again, he will draw blood from his opponents; then, ironically, Ray's own blood will be the cause of his downfall. Not long after we have graduated from Attica High School an imbalance of cells in the bloodstream will bring him down with a cross-block neither he nor anyone else, including his doting parents, will see coming. But at the moment Ray is robust as a fat hog in sunshine. At the moment he is my very good friend: shitbird, dipstick, numbnut.

Or, tired of tormenting Ray, I would improvise a song and sing it to the tractor, to the relentless sun or perhaps to the white birds skipping about in the furrow, feasting on insects and worms. I would sing the song until I had memorized it, and tonight, I'd tell myself, I'll try it on my girlfriend – and I would, but for some reason it would sound different, would lose something without the tractor and the sun and the squawking birds, so I'd cut it short and my girlfriend would smile, as if to say she approved of the shorter version, and we'd move on to something else.

Then one afternoon, in that increasingly narrow strip of ground yet to be plowed, I spotted a cottontail attempting to hide in a patch of stubble. I was feeling good because I could see the end of my endless job: Siberia, round by endless round, had been reduced to Oklahoma, then to Rhode Island, then to a plot that I'd be able to finish long before the merciless sun went down. One leg over the other the dog walks to Dover.

And I wondered how long the rabbit might remain there, in that narrow strip, before hightailing it across the plowed ground, how long it might cower in the stubble before the pop-pop-popping of the Johnny-popper – or maybe the realization that its meager protection was about to be plowed under – would force the cottontail into making a decision.

After several more rounds I made a decision of my own: I would catch the rabbit and take it home and in lieu of a song I would give the rabbit, as a gesture of my deep and abiding affection, to my girlfriend.

It is possible that my decision was prompted by the relentless sun's having fried my brain. This possibility, however, did not occur to me at the time. At the time I was riding a wave of elation. I was about to finish a task that at the start seemed truly endless, so I would soon be collecting a paycheck for more money than the job was worth, which in turn meant that I could buy a gadget for my darkroom or a new battery for my Philco portable or, hell yes, make a down payment on the moon. Boy howdy.

I stopped the tractor, shifted into neutral and jumped down. By now the unplowed patch was not much larger than, say, a couple of side-by-side end zones. My strategy was simple: I would chase the rabbit until I had exhausted it, then, with a length of binder twine from the toolbox I'd fashion a leash and secure my catch to a ball peen hammer from the same toolbox, hammer I'd dead-man in the soft earth until I finished the plowing. I had learned the art of dead-manning as a boy scout, had done it several times when the tent I was sleeping in was in danger of being blown away. You tie one end of a rope, or a length of twine, around an object like a tin can or a hammer handle, then you plant the object in a hole you have dug with your entrenching tool, a hole say somewhere between twelve to twenty inches deep. Finally, having packed the hole with whatever you removed to make the hole – dirt, sand, bunchgrass – you tie the other end of the leash to a grommet on the tent, or around the neck of a dead-tired cottontail, and sit back to await whatever storm or reward the future might deliver.

To have a perfect plan that is so pure and simple gives a person a genuine sense of satisfaction and pride, though the keen edge of such pleasure is somewhat dulled when there is no one present with whom to share the experience. You are alone at the center of a vast chunk of acreage, almost all of it plowed, your Johnny-popper popping idly in neutral, perhaps wondering what the hell you are up to; and, under a blistering late-July sun you are about to do what man has always done – capture an animal that in one way or another will enhance your relationship with a member of the opposite sex. You regret that you must do this without someone beside you, someone to give the experience the validation that later, should you survive, it so richly no doubt will deserve.

I approached the rabbit slowly and got surprisingly close before it ran and, filled with purpose, I ran also, assuming that the rabbit would not leave the unplowed part of the field and that sooner or later I would wear it down. I was not in the very best physical shape, to be honest; that would happen in the fall when my buddy Ray and I and the rest of the Bulldogs would do calisthenics and run wind sprints and in other ways prepare ourselves to confront the Bearcats from Harper and Pirates from Anthony and Indians from Medicine Lodge and Bluejays from Caldwell and Eagles from Kingman and Chieftains from Kiowa and Cardinals from Plainview, those Wichita hotdogs we would send to the showers soundly thumped. But I was not altogether out of shape, either, and I took pride in being something else, too: I was the higher animal.

Even so, the cottontail managed to elude me, chiefly because it could change directions so suddenly, until I was forced to remove my wide-brimmed hat and my shirt and revise my strategy: I would go to the toolbox once more, this time to remove a couple of box-end wrenches and the hammer I intended to use to dead-man one end of the leash. I would use these as ammunition, not to kill but to stun my prey, confident that one of my missiles would find its mark.

But now the cottontail zigged and zagged even more unpredictably than before, as if fully aware that I was armed with ammo from the toolbox – so aware, in fact, that it ran to the tractor where for several minutes it found cover, first behind a front wheel, then a rear one, until having decided that the idling John Deere could only serve as a temporary refuge it did what I had not expected: It left the patch of stubble and struck out across the vast expanse of soft plowed earth.

I did not break stride, though my pace slowed considerably when I hit the soft earth. I was wearing low-topped work boots, heavy enough under ideal conditions, and now feeling like dead weights, like big anvils. With each step one of these anvils sank deeply into the recently turned soil, and it required a lot of effort to pull one anvil from the soil so that I might then concentrate upon extracting the other. Ahead of me the rabbit seemed to have slowed its pace also, so if you were viewing the scene from atop a cloud, say, or a grain elevator, you might believe you were watching a pair of characters in a little drama, enacting their parts in slow motion – which in fact we were, though, at least for me, not voluntarily.

Now here is a curious thing: When I stopped to catch my breath, the cottontail, as if on cue, stopped also. I stood there breathing heavily, as the rabbit stopped and turned and looked at me; I was close enough to see that it was breathing maybe as heavily as I was and, had I been familiar with Henry David Thoreau's *Walden* I would have remembered his saying that *The hare, in its extremity, cries like a child.* So maybe it was possible that the rabbit, in this setting of plowed ground and hot sun, was as fatigued as its pursuer. In any case, having caught my breath I extracted a boot from the soil in which it had disappeared. At the same moment the cottontail moved one of its front legs and, as if in unison, we continued, in slow motion, to chase and to be chased.

Several times we paused to catch our mutual breaths, until finally I decided that if my mission were to be successful I must stop the rabbit from fleeing, must do this by throwing the hammer, and if necessary the box-end wrenches. I was several years away from becoming a lieutenant in the United States Marine Corps, so I knew nothing about the complex art of bracketing a target: firing one round beyond the target, another round short of it, and the third round – after a forward spotter had done the necessary calculations – smack in the center of the target.

So – ignorant of the complex art of bracketing, and having no forward spotter to advise me – I nonetheless proceeded on, taking careful aim and delivering the ball peen hammer. The cottontail had stopped at the moment I stopped, had turned on cue to look at me, and now it sat breathing heavily as the hammer sailed over its head and disappeared into the soft dark soil. I waited for a few moments then before dispatching one of the box-end wrenches. With the back of the hand that held the wrenches I wiped the sweat from my eyes. There was no breeze. When I looked at the rabbit, then beyond it, I could see heat waves rising and, beyond the waves, far beyond, a line of trees, a windbreak, moving with the motion of the waves.

The first box-end wrench lost itself in the plowed ground perhaps six feet to the cottontail's right, the second a trifle closer to its left. I was genuinely disappointed, because for three years in track I had been throwing the javelin and though I threw it for distance, not accuracy, I nonetheless believed that at such a short range I could hit anything, including a rabbit.

But I missed badly, and the chase ended in an odd way. I pursued the cottontail for only a few more minutes, until I could not move another step, not one, not if my life depended on it. And I believe that the cottontail was equally fatigued. I'm certain that had I been able to take the few steps to where the rabbit sat looking at me I could have picked it up without its moving a single muscle to resist – though, as Thoreau wrote, in its extremity it might have cried like a child.

I stood for a long time catching my breath and watching the line of trees in the distance shimmer behind a wall of heat waves. When finally I turned around and retraced my steps to the Johnny-popper, I felt too tired to look for the spent ammunition. Probably I would not have found it, anyway.

I put on my shirt and the wide-brimmed straw hat and boarded the tractor. In less than an hour I will have finished the job and will drive to the farmhouse where Ray's mother Lola will provide enough iced tea to float a battleship. I'll visit with her until Ray comes in from a different field, comes driving in at the wheel of a row-crop Farmall, steering with one hand and waving with the other, and, having showered under a garden hose we'll cruise into town in Ray's coupe and after a malt in the Rexall drugstore I'll call my girlfriend and when we meet I will tell her about the rabbit, and why I was chasing it, and she will tell me that she is glad I didn't catch it, that she'd rather have my good intentions than a live rabbit, you dipstick – applying one of the lovely epithets I taught her – any old day.

But at the moment I am about to finish the job, the John Deere crawling like an animal imbued with patience both unending and divine, and here is another curious thing: The cottontail has followed me back to the tractor, and there it is now, sitting nearby on a patch of stubble not much bigger than a postage stamp and looking for all the world like somebody's little brother playing King of the Mountain.

11

How shall I not love them, snoozing right through the Annunciation? They inhabit the outskirts of every importance.
                    —David Graham, "The Dogs in Dutch Paintings"

That's the thing about baseball . . . You do what they did before you. That's the connection you make . . . A man takes his kid to a game and thirty years later this is what they talk about when the poor old mutt's wasting away in the hospital.
                    —Don DeLillo, *Pafko at the Wall*

The child is father of the man;
And I could wish my days to be
Bound each to each by natural piety.
                    —William Wordsworth, "My Heart Leaps Up"

In Professor Loy Banks's composition class I chose to write an analysis of W. H. Auden's "Musee des Beaux Arts" because in a fit of bravado I believed that I could pronounce the title without the long bone-hard fingers of Dr. Minnie M. Miller rearranging my face. Fortunately, only the title was in French; the remainder of the poem was in English, which was close enough to American, or so I believed, to qualify.

Professor Banks had defined "analysis" as simply "a close look," and he wanted the look to be close enough to reveal something in the poem that we found objectionable. I was reluctant to do this. W. H. Auden was, and is, a highly respected poet, and at the time was very much alive, while I, though also alive, was one of the greenest nonentities on the face of this difficult earth. So as I wrote I postponed confronting my objection, which I had difficulty locating, until I neared the end of my paper. I had looked closely at the manner in which Auden in the first stanza treats the subject of human suffering, his referencing the "Old Masters" in general, saying that they knew the relative significance of suffering,

> how it takes place
> While someone is eating or opening a window or just walking
> dully along

and then in the second stanza, the final one, cites a specific example, a work by one of the "Old Masters," the Dutch painter Brueghel, how in "Icarus" he shows

> how everything turns away
> Quite leisurely from the disaster; the ploughman may
> Have heard the splash, the forsaken cry,

But for him it was not an important failure; the sun shone
As it had to on the white legs disappearing into the green
Water; and the expensive delicate ship that must have seen
Something amazing, a boy falling out of the sky,
Had somewhere to get to and sailed calmly on.

Of course I had to rely upon a footnote to tell me that Icarus, not heeding his father Daedalus's advice, had flown too close to the sun after he had escaped from the labyrinth, escape made possible by wings held on by wax, whereupon he falls to his death in the green sea. I praised the poem's compression without knowing much about compression, and the classical allusion without knowing much about either the classics or allusions. I stated that Auden's treatment of his subject indicates that he knows how difficult it is for a person to be sensitive to everyone else's misfortunes. All of us, I believe I said, have "somewhere to get to," and if we stop to mourn or acknowledge everyone else's miseries we might never get there.

My objection, such as it was, was to Auden's use of the word "behind" to denote the hindquarters of a horse. While something momentous is occurring, writes Auden, the horse "Scratches its innocent behind on a tree."

Behind? I had never heard anyone refer to a horse's rear end as its "behind." It seemed to me that the poet was being unduly euphemistic, not only because he called the horse's rear end its "behind," but also because this particular horse belonged to a man who earned his wage torturing his fellow human beings:

the torturer's horse
Scratches its innocent behind on a tree.

One must assume that a torturer's horse would have been a streetwise animal, that it would have witnessed many and varied forms of torture – poking out of eyes, drawings and quarterings and mutilations and slivers of bone up the nostrils – and would therefore be pretty much inured to the suffering of others, and in this convoluted sense free of blame, though probably "innocent" meant chiefly that the horse, while present at the awful events, had not instigated or taken part in them. Such an animal might be expected to scratch itself where the itch occurred, but the poet should not call this spot the horse's "behind." The word is too polite.

So in its place, having girded my loins with audacity, I suggested "rump." (Yes, I had considered other possibilities, among them "bottom" and "butt" and, in deference to Dr. Minnie M. Miller, "derriere"; certainly I thought about "rear end," a term in my limited lexicon I cherished because I associated it with the title Mother had assigned those many years ago to my favorite family photograph, the delightful "Sumner's rear end.") But finally "rump" won out. Yes, "rump" it should be: "Scratches its innocent rump on a tree." Rump was neither too harsh nor too delicate. It was in fact the word my paternal grandfather called the posterior of his own horses, or his grandson's arse if he had done something amiss, which once in a great while I suppose he did, though Grandfather never went beyond a threat – "I'll tan your little rump." In any case, I was aware of how Grandfather influenced my preference for "rump" and thus my objection to "behind."

Professor Banks appreciated the objection, he said, but he told me that "behind" was distinctly if not uniquely British, and W. H. Auden *was* British, meaning I guess that to the British sensibility "behind" was somehow the equivalent of "rump." I tried my best to understand what Loy Banks was saying, but my preference for "rump" nonetheless lingers.

I had come to the writing of my analysis meagerly equipped. In class we had discussed a couple of poems, Edwin Arlington

Robinson's "Mr. Flood's Party" and Edgar Lee Masters's "Lucinda Matlock"; and of course Vachel Lindsay's "Abraham Lincoln Walks at Midnight" yet haunted my memory, as did Edna St. Vincent Millay's "Dirge Without Music." These were legitimate credentials, but they were not extensive. I was familiar with some pieces that might loosely be regarded as poetry, among them some off-color verse – *A shepherd boy lay in the grass, his faithful dog right by his ass,* for example – and I knew a number of limericks that floated about in the public domain when I was younger, if by domain one means the pool hall and the barber shop and the Champlin filling station, where each evening after school I sat folding sixty-seven *Wichita Beacon*s, and I had memorized the only two lines of poetry I ever heard my father recite:

> The boy stood on the burning deck,
> Eating peanuts by the peck.

So I had approached the Auden poem with an impressive reservoir of inadequacy. My earlier essays, according to Professor Banks, had succeeded, and because they were based upon personal experiences, I wrote them with more than a mustard seed of confidence. The John Deere essays had been especially well received, and what I wanted was to remain with the John Deere, or any number of its relatives, and cultivate, so to speak, that terrain which thus far had borne fruit – cultivate it, perhaps, indefinitely. But education does not work that way, and of course it shouldn't. So at my professor's urging I wandered into new territory, the strange and compelling realm of poetry, which included analysis, which in turn can lead one down the slippery slopes of diction and nuance – of *behind* and *rear end* and *rump* and Englishmen who I secretly thought did not have the brains they were born with or, if they did, didn't know how to use them.

Without my fully realizing it, during my first term in college Professor Loy Banks had sparked in me a lifelong interest in writing and literature. But it was not until the fall semester of the next year, when taking a somewhat more advanced literature class, that I decided what I wanted to do; and, oddly enough, I think I first began to realize the true extent of my interest when I elected not to cut Professor Wyrick's contemporary literature class to listen to a baseball game I very much wanted to hear.

Never before had I allowed something as trivial as formal education to come between me and a Dodger baseball game, but I admired Professor Wyrick and did not want to miss out on anything he said. And on that day the class was about to tackle a poem that Professor Wyrick said – no, *emphasized* – was difficult but very important in the development of American letters. I had written down that phrase, "American letters." I had never heard "letters" used as a synonym for "literature" or "writing." Well, shitfire, on paper I was a sophomore – but I was still a greenhorn, still an ill-equipped south-central Kansas hayseed who no doubt would spend the rest of his hayseed life trying to catch up. I had passed Dr. Minnie M. Miller's French classes, but hardly with distinction; my diligence over two semesters earned me ten hours of C and a face that even now can feel the impression of that grand woman's bony fingers. *Muh-shoe. Muh-shoe. Muh-shoe.* And I had passed biology too, or rather endured it, my professor either exceptionally compassionate or wholly unable to compute figures, my highest score somewhere between what one of the locals back home in the pool hall or barber shop might have called *low* and *low-down.*

Professor Wyrick was a tall, angular, reddish-haired man with a well-manicured mustache and a wry sense of humor – Errol Flynn minus the dimples. He was a smoker but he did not smoke in the classroom. He was never without a tie and coat, though the one was seldom snugged and the other, whether the brown tweed or the green, was somewhat frayed at the elbows. Standing or sitting, he kept his back impressively straight. He seemed aristocratic without being pompous, removed but not altogether distant.

So here is the scene: a classroom on the fourth floor of the administration building on the campus of a small teachers college in Kansas. Early afternoon in early October. Sun off and on highlighting windows that line the south wall. The room is not filled because some of the students, less dedicated than the hayseed, are somewhere listening to the ball game, some in fact sitting out in the hall bending their ears to a portable radio. The hallway of course is thick with smoke – *Lucky Strike, so round, so firm, so fully packed, so free and easy on the draw.* At home I had been listening to the game myself, listening over the old Philco my mother had made the final payment on, half jittery and half smug because the Dodgers had an early lead and their ace, Don Newcombe, was surely equal to the Giants' ace, Sal Maglie. But in baseball, they say, no lead is a safe lead. In baseball the game isn't over, someone eventually will say, until it's over.

Why favor the Dodgers? Because Urie the barber favored them. Because Urie said that in the beginning God created the National League, and within that league His most cherished nine were the Bums from Brooklyn. Because Pistol Pete Reiser had been a center fielder for the Dodgers, and Reiser was probably the fiercest competitor, Urie said, that ever donned a jockstrap. Because, attempting to snag balls hit too far to be caught, Pistol Pete ran into an assortment of walls – stone and board and ivy-covered brick – and suffered so goddamn many concussions that eventually he would have to be moved out of center field and into management. Because . . .

I sat in the desk chair closest to the door, hoping that Professor Wyrick would not close the door, hoping that with the door open I could hear enough of the game from the student's portable to stay updated. And my hope, so very nearly a prayer, was answered. Our professor, tall and lean and stately, entered the room, his pale blue copy of our anthology, *This Generation*, in his left hand. And he did not close the door.

Professor Wyrick, perhaps because he too liked baseball and did not want to penalize those who chose the game over the class, did not call the roll, but moved directly into a discussion of that difficult but very important poem in the development of American letters, T. S. Eliot's "The Love Song of J. Alfred Prufrock." I had read the poem a couple of times, each reading confirming the first half of Professor Wyrick's contention: The poem was indeed, at least for me, very difficult, and the difficulty began with the title. Love song? How could this possibly be? Isn't Mr. Prufrock dejected and indecisive and bewildered? At one point he says, "It is impossible to say just what I mean!" And he laments, "I should have been a pair of ragged claws / Scuttling across the floors of silent seas."

What I could hear beyond the open door, by cupping a hand to my left ear, was mostly a confusion of murmur and subdued babbling, though once in a while a word or so came to me clearly enough to be recognized: *Reese swings, Dark reaches, Mays camps under, Maglie winds up* . . . Because I had waited until the last minute to leave home for class I knew not only that the Dodgers were leading, but also that they had avoided potential disaster in the bottom of the second inning – thanks to Bobby Thomson, who went to second not noticing that the base already was occupied by Whitey Lockman. So Thomson was tagged out, thus squelching that second-inning threat by the Giants. But what

211

might be happening just now, somewhere, I guessed, around the fifth or sixth, or maybe even seventh, inning?

Professor Wyrick spoke for some time about what he called the mood of the poem, how Eliot had established it with his opening simile; the evening, wrote the poet – the evening that Prufrock and his invited guest, the reader, are about to take a stroll together – is "spread out against the sky / Like a patient etherized upon a table . . ." *Etherized upon a table.* Professor Wyrick spoke this phrase in a voice decidedly italic. To be etherized, Professor Wyrick said, is to be both alive and not alive, to be breathing but unable to function otherwise as a productive human being. And what is the mood? Rather gloomy, students, don't you think? I had assumed, after that narrow escape at the bottom of the second, that good luck in this third of a three-game series was riding with the Dodgers and would continue to stay with them. Win this one, Dodgers, and the pennant is yours – no, *ours.* They had played one hundred and fifty-four games and two playoff contests and it had come down to this final confrontation. Win this one and they'd own – *we'd* own – the National League pennant.

Beyond the open door smoke hung like a wispy screen of cirrus in the hallway. *So round, so firm, so fully packed, so free and easy on the draw.* And for several innings I had been correct, though I'd have to wait until later to learn it: The Dodger luck was holding. In the bottom of the seventh the Giants would tie the score at one all, but the Dodgers would regain the lead at the top of the ninth, 4–1. Boy howdy.

My classmates and I meanwhile strolled with J. Alfred Prufrock "through certain half-deserted streets, / The muttering retreats / Of restless nights in one-night cheap hotels . . ." Fortunately, Professor Wyrick was strolling with us, raising questions that his students struggled mightily to answer, and as one of these students I

212

must admit I was beginning to feel an affinity with Prufrock, so when he says, "I am pinned and wriggling on the wall," says it in the calm, deliberate voice of Professor Wyrick, I nod sympathetically, thinking, J. Alfred, I know exactly what you mean.

Now Professor Wyrick was not an actor by trade, but he had some thespian in him. He enjoyed reading to his class, standing tall with an open book in his left hand as his long right arm with its long-fingered hand moved in fluid gestures, movements so sweeping and delicate that it was difficult not to study the gestures at the expense of listening to the words. I was in a precarious position, listening to Professor Wyrick with one ear while trying to hear the radio in the hallway with the other (Prufrock wondering where to part his hair versus Duke Snider, or was it Robinson, taking a pitch, or was he swinging?), watching the liquid movements of the professor's arm – today it was hidden inside a length of brown tweed coat – then looking from time to time through the open door to the smoke in the hallway, smoke that was thickening as additional students began to gather for their three o'clock classes.

The sad truth is that, in spite of the cupped hand at my ear, I could hear very little beyond a small drone from the radio; to keep myself informed about the game I had to rely upon imagination bolstered by faith and hope. Another sad truth is that, having unlocked the door to our understanding of Eliot's important contribution to American letters, an unlocking that included some comments on the irony implicit in the poem's title, Professor Wyrick left the door significantly ajar – that is, he returned to the opening lines of the poem and began to half read, half recite until two things dawned upon me: (1) in two minutes, by my watch, the class period would be over, and (2) Professor Wyrick did not intend to dismiss us until he had performed "The Love Song of J. Alfred Prufrock" from its first line through its last.

How does one resign oneself to what cannot be resigned to? I studied the smoke in the hallway as Professor Wyrick accompanied J. Alfred Prufrock through "sawdust restaurants with oyster-shells"; I watched and with one ear listened to gaggles of students as they added to and navigated the hallway smoke; I closed my eyes and saw Don Newcombe take the sign from Campanella, then deliver a fastball that crossed the inside of home plate only an inch or so from Monte Irvin's chin. Christ! Can you imagine? Not many weeks ago the shit-heel Giants were thirteen games out of first place. Now here they were at the Polo Grounds playing for the National League pennant – one final playoff game, winner take all.

> In the room the women come and go
> Talking of Michelangelo.

Professor Wyrick seemed oblivious to everything but his performance, which under other circumstances would have been impressive. But the Dodgers, *my* Brooklyn Dodgers, were playing to win the pennant – didn't our professor know? – and besides, according to my watch the class period was officially over. Yes, indeed,

> I should have been a pair of ragged claws
> Scuttling across the floors of silent seas.

I had to admit to myself that the Dodgers had experienced their own share of good luck: They too had ended the regular season with a dramatic flourish, defeating the Phillies 9–8 in a fourteen-inning marathon.

> Praise God from whom all blessings flow.
> Praise Him for Rube Walker and Carl Furillo,

and praise Him especially for Jackie Robinson, who blasted the game-winning solo homer, an outright virtuoso performance.

And praise the Lord also that Professor Wyrick was about to conclude his perambulation with J. Alfred Prufock. Was I the only one in the classroom squirming? No, not by a long shot. Others too were checking their watches; in only a few minutes the next class would begin, and no doubt some of my fellow students, those who had to go to other buildings, would not be there on time.

It is fortuitous – I believe that's the word – that immediately after Professor Wyrick spoke the final line of "Prufrock," "Till human voices wake us, and we drown," all hell broke loose. Our professor must have believed that the eruption was in response to his performance, the outburst being too timely and too spontaneous to be otherwise. In any case, Professor Wyrick smiled; but before the smile had time to run its full course the classroom had emptied, I having more or less led the charge, and I was well into the process of being squeezed or trampled to death in the hallway when I heard that the Giants had won the pennant on a Thomson home run off Ralph Branca. But I did not believe it – because many of the students were laughing, as if they were happy. I didn't believe that, either. Happy? It is one thing for God to demonstrate His infinite capacity for injustice, as He often does; but it is quite something else for so many of His misbegotten creatures to be overjoyed about it.

I gripped my copy of *This Generation* and, disbelieving, fled from the building and into the chilly – and immortal – October air.

And now, remembering, it seems as if what I wanted to concentrate upon in college became clear on that day when Professor Wyrick took us for a walk with J. Alfred Prufrock at the same time Bobby Thomson hit the "shot heard 'round the world," as his home run ultimately was labeled. At any rate, from then on I began to feel confident about what I wanted to do: Perhaps the hayseed could become a student.

And here is another reason why I decided to become something more than a south-central Kansas bumpkin: I wanted to set an example for my brother, whose little ass on so many occasions I had kicked squarely into the middle of next Wednesday. He was a superior student, much brighter than I ever hoped to be, and he was personable beyond description; but he had a tendency to hide his brightness under a bushel basket and, as it struggled for oxygen, he'd cut classes and smoke cigarettes and raise Cain and indulge other nonacademic activities, some if not most of them intended to impress those members of the opposite sex who found both his charm and his antics irresistible.

At the time, Johnny favored the New York Yankees, another transgression I felt obliged less to forgive than to correct. And at the time – one year before he would need to decide whether to enroll in college or remain at home to continue his glamorous indiscretions – he was living with our father in a little apartment in what we called a rooming house, our mother having decided to leave. It had not been a very friendly separation, but probably inevitable, given my mother's desire to construct ladders with far too many rungs for my father to climb. She therefore left for the big city, for Wichita, with a longtime lady friend she admired and trusted.

For more than one reason, then, I determined to set an example – for myself, for my brother, for all those other hayseeds who didn't know shit from Shinola but who nonetheless, like the figures in Brueghel's painting, had "somewhere to get to." I attended classes as dutifully as if I had been carrying a calf bucket filled with dirt up earthen steps and across a gravel driveway to dump on a patch of bunchgrass just east of the outhouse, or pushing a wheelbarrow half filled with Zenda, Kansas, soil up an incline to be deposited under the sprawling limbs of an elm tree. I was taking my courses one stride at a time, one leg over the other, and I especially looked forward to my comparative literature class. Sitting in a classroom three days a week, I'd anticipate Professor Wyrick's entering the room to begin the discussion of a story or a play or poem, or to review a set of papers he'd return at the end of the hour; and there was always something fresh and invigorating about it, something warmly anticipatory, Professor Wyrick commenting and asking questions in a soft, measured voice that once in a while reminded me of my father's voice when occasionally he'd attempt a song: *What a beautiful thought I am thinking, concerning the great speckled bird*, or the acceptance I heard in his voice that night we walked home from Virginia Mae Prindle's house where I had left the yellow lunch bucket: *I'm saving up coupons to buy one of those. A coupon redeemer, I'll die, I suppose.*

I suppose. But not just now. Because just now Professor Wyrick is entering the room, and one's thoughts of doing anything short of living at least until the end of the hour must be postponed.